A Comprehensive Guide to

A Compre

COLLECTING RARE ERROR COINS in 2024

Learn how to Identify, Value, and profit from your error coins

Peter S. Elliott

Disclaimer:

"The Comprehensive Guide to Collecting Rare Error Coins in 2024" is provided for informational and educational purposes only. While we strive to ensure the accuracy of the information, the world of coin collecting is ever-evolving, and coin values may fluctuate. The content is not intended as financial or investment advice, and readers should conduct their own research and seek professional guidance for any financial decisions. Coin collecting and trading may involve risks, and individuals should exercise caution. The author and publisher are not responsible for any actions taken based on the information provided in the guide.

TABLE OF CONTENTS

PREFACE

Welcome to "Collecting Rare Error Coins." This book is all about exploring the fascinating world of collecting coins that are different or unusual. It's like going on a treasure hunt!

Let me tell you a story that inspired this book. One day, a friend of mine bought a $5 gold coin from someone who said they needed money for their family. But this wasn't just any coin – it was special and mysterious. We couldn't figure out if it was real or not, so we spent a lot of time trying to find out more about it. We even contacted experts, but no one could give us a clear answer.

This story got me thinking about all the interesting coins out there and the stories behind them. That's why I wrote this book – to share the excitement of collecting rare coins and uncovering their secrets.

In "Collecting Rare Error Coins," you'll learn about different types of unusual coins, how to spot them, and the thrill of discovering something unique. Whether you're a beginner or an experienced collector, I hope this book sparks your curiosity and inspires you to explore the world of rare coins.

So, join me on this journey as we dive into the fascinating world of Numismatist. Let's uncover the hidden treasures and enjoy the adventure together!

GUESS YOU FOUND A NEW HOBBY

Finding Peace in a Busy World

Life gets really busy sometimes, doesn't it? With work, family, and everything else we have going on, it's easy to feel overwhelmed. But you know what? We all need something to help us relax and take a break from the craziness. That's where hobbies come in, like collecting coins!

You know those shiny pieces of metal we use to buy stuff? Yeah, those are coins! They're literally everywhere – in our pockets, on the ground, even hiding in our couch cushions. You can get them from almost anywhere you use cash. And guess what? You only need a few – or even just one – to start collecting and go on a super cool journey into the world of coins.

So, how do people get into collecting coins? Well, it usually starts with finding a weird or old coin by accident. Maybe it's in your pocket change or a friend gives it to you. That's when the magic happens! You start wondering about that coin and wanting to find more like it. It's like a treasure hunt that never gets old!

Collecting coins isn't just a hobby – it's a way to escape from the stresses of everyday life. When things get tough, diving into the world of coins can be a calming escape. It's like going on an adventure where you can learn cool stuff and forget about your worries for a while.

In a world that's always go, go, go, it's important to take time for yourself. For many people, collecting coins is a way to do just that. It's not just about having fun – it's about finding balance and doing something you love. So, keep collecting those coins and hold onto the things that make you happy!

Collecting coins is about more than just finding cool stuff – it's about finding peace and happiness in a world that can sometimes feel crazy. So, keep hunting for those treasures and enjoying the simple pleasures that coins bring. After all, in a busy world, finding peace through hobbies is pretty special.

INTRODUCTION

Error coins are a fascinating and unique category of coins that have become highly sought after by collectors and investors alike. Unlike regular coins, error coins possess some form of anomaly or mistake during the minting process, making them distinct and valuable. These errors can occur due to various factors, such as mechanical malfunctions, human error, or even intentional alterations. The presence of these errors adds a layer of intrigue and rarity to the coins, making them highly desirable among numismatists.

Error coins can be found in various denominations, including pennies, nickels, dimes, quarters, and even silver and gold coins. The errors themselves can take on many forms, ranging from minor imperfections to major deviations from the intended design. Some common types of errors include off-center strikes, double dies, clipped planchets, broad strikes, and brockages, among others. Each type of error coin has its own unique characteristics and value, which we will explore in more detail throughout this book.

The appeal of error coins lies not only in their rarity but also in the stories they tell. Each error coin has its own narrative, representing a momentary lapse in the minting process or a unique event that occurred during production. These coins serve as a tangible reminder of the intricate and complex nature of coin production, making them highly collectible for those interested in the history and artistry of numismatics.

It is important to note that not all mistakes or anomalies on coins qualify as error coins. Some imperfections, such as scratches, dents, or wear from circulation, are considered damage rather than errors. Error coins, on the other hand, are the result of mistakes made during the minting process itself. These errors can range from minor variations in design elements to major deviations that significantly alter the appearance of the coin.

Collecting error coins can be a rewarding and profitable endeavor. As with any collectible, the value of error coins is determined by various factors, including the rarity of the error, the demand among collectors, and the overall condition of the coin. In this book, we will delve into the intricacies of identifying, valuing, and profiting from error coins, providing you with the knowledge and tools necessary to build a successful collection.

Knowing error coins is crucial whether you are a novice collector or an experienced collector. A piece of history may be acquired by collectors with these unusual and fascinating coins, which also provide an insight into the world of coin manufacture. We will examine mistake coin kinds, their historical relevance, and methods for recognizing and appraising them in the upcoming chapters. You'll be equipped with the knowledge and skills necessary to successfully navigate the world of mistake coin collecting by the conclusion of this book, and you could even turn a profit. So come along with me as we begin on this thrilling adventure to learn how to gather uncommon coin mistakes and turn a profit.

Why Collect Error Coins?

Collecting coins has been a popular hobby for centuries, with enthusiasts drawn to the beauty, history, and rarity of these small pieces of metal. While many collectors focus on acquiring coins in pristine condition, there is a subset of collectors who are captivated by the allure of error coins. These unique and often rare coins have defects or anomalies that occurred during the minting process, making them highly sought after by collectors and investors alike.

One of the primary reasons to collect error coins is their historical significance. These coins provide a hint into the manufacturing process of the mint and the potential challenges faced during production. Each error coin tells a story of a mistake or anomaly that occurred, making it a tangible piece of history. By collecting error coins, you become a custodian of these artifacts, preserving them for future generations to appreciate and study.

Rarity and Exclusivity

The rarity and exclusivity of error coins add to their appeal and value. As a collector, the joy of finding a rare error coin can be exciting, and the sense of accomplishment in adding it to your collection is unmatched.

Unique Aesthetics

Error coins often possess unique and visually striking characteristics that set them apart from regular coins. These anomalies can include off-center strikes, double dies, clipped planchets, and other fascinating errors. The unconventional appearance of error coins adds an element of intrigue and beauty to any collection. The distinctiveness of these coins makes them stand out and creates a visually captivating display.

Investment Potential

Beyond the joy of collecting, error coins can also be a profitable investment. The rarity and desirability of certain error coins can drive up their market value significantly over time. As more collectors and investors enter the market, the demand for error coins continues to grow. By carefully selecting and acquiring error coins with potential, collectors can enjoy both the aesthetic pleasure of their collection and the potential financial gains.

Educational Value

Collecting error coins is not only a hobby but also an educational pursuit. It provides an opportunity to learn about the intricacies of the minting process, the different types of errors, and the history behind each coin. By studying error coins, collectors can develop a deep understanding of numismatics and gain insights into the evolution of coin production. This knowledge can be shared with others, fostering a sense of community and camaraderie among fellow collectors.

Thrill of the Hunt

For many collectors, the thrill of the hunt is a significant factor in collecting error coins. Searching through pocket change, bank rolls, and coin rolls in the hopes of finding a rare error coin can be an exciting and rewarding experience. The element of surprise and the anticipation of discovering a valuable error coin add an element of adventure to the hobby. The joy of finding a hidden gem in everyday circulation is a feeling that only collectors can truly appreciate.

Connection to the Past

Error coins provide a tangible connection to the past. Each coin carries a piece of history, whether it be a misaligned die, a double strike, or a clipped planchet. By collecting error coins, you are preserving a part of the minting process that would otherwise be lost to time. These coins serve as a reminder of the craftsmanship and artistry that went into their creation, and the errors they bear are a testament to the imperfections of human endeavor.

The History of Error Coins

The history of error coins is a fascinating journey that spans centuries. These unique and valuable coins have captivated collectors and numismatists for generations. Understanding the origins and evolution of error coins can provide valuable insights into their significance and appeal.

The existence of error coins can be traced back to the earliest days of coin production. In ancient times, when coins were struck by hand, errors were more common due to the manual nature of the minting process. These errors included off-center strikes, double strikes, and planchet errors.

One notable example of an early error coin is the "widow's mite" from the time of the New Testament. These small bronze coins were often struck off-center, resulting in irregular shapes and designs. Despite their imperfections, these coins hold great historical and religious significance.

Error Coins in the Modern Era

The production of error coins continued into the modern era with the advent of mechanized coin minting. As technology advanced, new types of errors emerged, including double dies, clipped planchets, and brockages.

One of the most famous modern error coins is the 1955 doubled die Lincoln cent. This coin features a noticeable doubling of the obverse design, creating a distinct and sought-after variety. The 1955 doubled die cent is highly valued by collectors and is considered a key date in the Lincoln cent series.

The Role of Error Coins in Numismatic History

Error coins have played a significant role in the field of numismatics throughout history. They have provided valuable insights into the minting process, quality control measures, and the evolution of coin production techniques.

In some cases, error coins have led to improvements in minting technology and quality control. Minting errors often prompt mints to reevaluate their processes and make necessary adjustments to prevent future errors. This continuous improvement has resulted in more precise and accurate coin production over time.

The Popularity and Collectability of Error Coins

The popularity of error coins among collectors has grown steadily over the years. Collectors are drawn to the uniqueness and rarity of these coins, as well as the challenge of finding and identifying them. Error coins offer a thrilling and rewarding collecting experience, as each discovery can be a treasure hunt in itself.

The value of error coins is determined by various factors, including the type and severity of the error, the rarity of the coin, and the demand among collectors. Some error coins can command significant premiums, especially if they are in high demand or are part of a popular series.

Notable Error Coin Discoveries

Throughout history, there have been several notable error coin discoveries that have captured the attention of collectors and the general public. These discoveries have often resulted in increased interest and demand for error coins.

One such discovery occurred in 2004 when a Wisconsin state quarter was found with an extra leaf on the ear of corn on the reverse design. This error, known as the "Extra Leaf Wisconsin Quarter," created a frenzy among collectors, with some examples selling for thousands of dollars.

Another famous error coin is the 1943 copper cent. During World War II, copper was in high demand for the war effort, and the U.S. Mint switched to using zinc-coated steel for cent production. However, a small number of copper cents were mistakenly struck, making them extremely rare and valuable.

The Future of Error Coin Collecting

As technology continues to advance, the production of error coins may become less common. Automated quality control measures and improved minting processes have significantly reduced the occurrence of errors in modern coin production.

However, the allure of error coins will always remain. The thrill of finding a rare and valuable error coin will continue to attract collectors and enthusiasts. As new generations of collectors emerge, the demand for error coins may evolve, leading to new discoveries and opportunities in the field.

Chapter 1

FRAMEWORK OF A COIN

The obverse

The obverse of a coin, also known as the front or heads side, usually displays a design like a portrait or emblem representing the issuing authority, such as a government or monarch.

The reverse

The reverse side, or tails side, of a coin typically has a different design from the obverse. It might feature imagery like national symbols, historical events, or cultural motifs.

LEGEND
DEVICE
DENTILS
RIM
FIELD
DATE

MOTTO
LEGEND
DEVICE
MINT MARK
DENOMINATION
EDGE

Edge: The edge of a coin is the outer border or rim that goes around its outside. It can be plain, have grooves, letters, or designs on it. Sometimes, mint marks showing where the coin was made are found on the edge.

Field: The field is the flat or slightly curved surface on the front and back of the coin, without any raised designs or writing. It's like a background for the main pictures and writing.

Devices: Devices are the raised parts on the coin's surface, like pictures, words, and symbols. On the front, they might include portraits or emblems, while on the back, they could show national symbols or important events.

Legend: The legend is the writing on the coin, such as the country's name, value, and other important details. It's usually around the edge of the coin but can also be part of the design.

Mint Mark: The mint mark is a small symbol or letter that shows where the coin was made. It can be on the front, back, or edge of the coin.

Mint Mark	Description
P	Philadelphia Mint
D	Denver Mint
S	San Francisco Mint
W	West Point Mint
CC	Carson City Mint (historic)
O	New Orleans Mint (historic)

These mint marks indicate the location where the coin was produced by the United States Mint.

Rim: The rim of a coin is the raised border that encircles the outer edge of both the obverse and reverse sides.

Differentiating Coin's Edge from Rim

Numismatists, scholars, and collectors of currency often refer to the heads side as the 'obverse' and the tails side as the 'reverse.' The 'edge' is specifically the part visible when looking at a coin sideways, separating the obverse from the reverse and running along the coin's entire circumference.

Significance of Coin Edges

The edge design serves multiple purposes, including aesthetics, functionality, and security. It can enhance the coin's appearance, carry inscriptions or ornamentation, and play a crucial role in preventing counterfeiting and unauthorized alteration of coins.

Types of Coin Edges

1. **Plain Edge**: Smooth and uniform, devoid of any design.

2. **Reeded Edge**: Characterized by a series of grooves or ridges, commonly found on certain denominations.

3. **Lettered Edge**: Features inscriptions such as dates, mint marks, or mottos.

4. **Decorated Edge**: Elaborate designs such as flowers or vines adorn this type of edge.

5. **Grooved Edge**: Contains a deep score or groove encircling the coin's circumference.

6. **Security Edge**: Utilizes a combination of different edge designs to enhance the coin's security measures.

Differentiating Edge from Rim

It's essential to differentiate between the edge and the rim of a coin. While the rim is the raised flat part encircling the perimeter on both sides of the coin, the edge runs along the coin's circumference, separating the obverse and reverse.

Practical Purposes of Coin Edges

Beyond aesthetics, coin edges play practical roles. They assist visually impaired individuals in distinguishing between coins of different denominations and provide tactile feedback for all users when handling coins.

Tools and Techniques for Identifying Errors

Identifying error coins can be an exciting and rewarding process for collectors. It requires a keen eye for detail and a good understanding of the various types of errors that can occur during the minting process.

Magnification Tools

One of the most essential tools for identifying errors in coins is a magnification device. A magnifying glass or a loupe with a magnification power of at least 5x is recommended for examining the finer details of a coin. This will allow you to closely inspect the surfaces, edges, and lettering of the coin, where errors are often found.

For more advanced collectors, a digital microscope or a jeweler's loupe with higher magnification power can be used to examine coins in even greater detail. These tools can reveal minute errors that may not be visible to the naked eye, such as doubled dies or repunched mint marks.

Lighting

Proper lighting is crucial when examining coins for errors. A well-lit area with natural or artificial light can help reveal the subtle details that may indicate an error. Avoid using harsh or direct lighting, as it can create shadows and make it difficult to spot errors.

To enhance the visibility of errors, you can use a small flashlight or a desk lamp with an adjustable arm to direct light onto the coin from different angles. This technique can help highlight any irregularities in the coin's surface, such as doubling or missing elements.

Coin Grading Guides

Understanding the grading system used for coins is crucial when identifying and valuing error coins. Coin grading guides, such as the Official ANA Grading Standards for United States Coins, provide a standardized framework for assessing the condition and quality of a coin.

By familiarizing yourself with the grading terminology and criteria, you will be able to determine the level of preservation and wear on a coin. This knowledge is particularly important when evaluating error coins, as certain errors may affect the overall grade and value of the coin.

Comparison and Attribution

Comparing coins and attributing errors can be a valuable technique for identifying errors. By comparing a coin to known examples of error coins, you can quickly spot any deviations or anomalies. This can be done by examining similar coins in your collection, consulting reference books, or using online resources.

When attributing errors, it is important to consider the specific characteristics of the error, such as the type, location, and extent of the error. This information can help you determine the rarity and value of the error coin.

Online Communities and Forums

Engaging with online communities and forums dedicated to error coin collecting can be an invaluable resource for identifying errors. These platforms allow collectors to share their knowledge, experiences, and images of error coins.

By actively participating in these communities, you can learn from experienced collectors, seek advice on identifying specific errors, and even showcase your own discoveries. The collective expertise and enthusiasm of these communities can greatly enhance your understanding of error coins and help you build a valuable collection. Some communities to join -

https://www.money.org/

https://www.nlgonline.org/

Central States Numismatic Society

Step-by-Step Coin Production Process

Step One: Blanking

Blanks, flat metal discs that will become coins, are produced for various denominations including nickels, dimes, quarters, half dollars, and dollars. The Mint purchases coils of metal tailored to each denomination's specifications. These coils are fed through a machine that straightens the metal before entering a blanking press. The press punches out blanks at a rate of up to 14,000 per minute. The blanks have a slightly different diameter but the same thickness as finished coins.

Step Two: Annealing

Blanks undergo annealing to prepare them for striking. Annealing involves heating the blanks to temperatures up to 1,600 degrees Fahrenheit in an oxygen-free environment to prevent tarnishing. After heating, the blanks are rapidly cooled in a quench tank filled with a mixture of water, citric acid powder, and lubricants. Machines lift the blanks from the tank to drain, ensuring they do not stick together.

Step Three: Washing & Drying

The annealed blanks are washed to restore their original color using a cleaning solution containing cleaning and anti-tarnish agents. They are then steam-dried before moving to the next stage.

Step Four: Upsetting

Blanks are fed into an upsetting mill, where they are subjected to a groove slightly narrower than their diameter. This process raises the metal around the edge, forming a rim. The rim protects the final coin from wear and facilitates stacking. Blanks with rims are known as planchets. Some planchets undergo additional burnishing for special finishes.

Step Five: Striking

Planchets move to coin presses for striking. The presses force obverse and reverse dies together against the planchet, imprinting both sides of the coin simultaneously. Collars around the planchet prevent excessive metal expansion and form the edge design. Circulating coin presses can strike up to 750 coins per minute, producing millions of coins daily. Samples are inspected for errors before packaging.

Step Six: Bagging & Packaging

Circulating coins are counted, weighed, and dumped into bulk storage bags. The bags are weighed and stored until distribution to Federal Reserve Banks. Numismatic coins are packaged into blister packs, lenses, or other packaging by robots and automated machines. Some coins are packaged by hand. Bullion coins are packed in monster boxes for shipment to authorized dealers.

Grading and Authenticating Error Coins

Grading and authenticating error coins is an essential step in the collecting process. It ensures that the coin's condition and authenticity are accurately assessed, which is crucial for determining its value and potential profitability. In this section, we will explore the importance of grading and authenticating error coins and discuss the various grading systems and authentication methods used in the numismatic community.

The Importance of Grading

Grading error coins involves evaluating their condition and assigning a grade that reflects their overall state of preservation. The grade of a coin plays a significant role in determining its value, as higher-grade coins generally command higher prices in the market. Grading error coins can be particularly challenging due to the unique nature of their errors, which may affect different aspects of the coin's appearance.

Accurate grading is crucial for collectors and investors alike. Collectors seek error coins in the best possible condition to enhance the visual appeal of their collections. Investors, on the other hand, rely on grading to assess the potential return on their investment. A well-graded error coin can attract more buyers and potentially yield a higher profit when sold.

Grading Systems

Several grading systems are used in the numismatic community to assess the condition of coins. The most widely recognized and respected grading system is the Sheldon Scale, also known as the American Numismatic Association (ANA) grading scale. This scale assigns a numerical grade ranging from 1 to 70 to coins, with 70 being the highest grade representing a perfectly preserved coin.

When grading error coins, it is essential to consider both the error and the overall condition of the coin. The error itself does not determine the grade; instead, it is evaluated alongside other factors such as strike quality, luster, surface preservation, and eye appeal. Graders assess the coin's overall appearance, taking into account any wear, scratches, or other imperfections that may affect its grade.

Coins are typically graded on a scale from Poor to Mint State (MS), with various grades in between. Here's a breakdown:

1. **Poor (P)**: Coins in poor condition are heavily worn and may have significant damage, making identification difficult. They are often barely recognizable.

2. **Fair (F)**: Fair condition coins also have heavy wear, with most details worn smooth. However, major features are still distinguishable.

3. **Good (G)**: Coins in good condition have extensive wear, with most details worn flat but major features still visible.

4. **Very Good (VG)**: Very good condition coins show heavy wear, with major details visible but somewhat flattened.

5. **Fine (F)**: Coins in fine condition exhibit moderate to considerable wear but still have legible details and designs.

6. **Very Fine (VF)**: Very fine condition coins show moderate wear on the high points of the design but retain most major details.

7. **Extremely Fine (EF or XF)**: Extremely fine condition coins may have light wear on the high points of the design but still retain most of their original detail.

8. **About Uncirculated (AU)**: Coins in AU condition may show very slight traces of wear on the highest points of the design due to handling or minor contact with other coins.

9. **Mint State (MS)**: Mint state coins are those that have never been in circulation and exhibit no signs of wear or damage. They are assigned numerical grades on a scale from MS-60 to MS-70, with MS-70 being the highest grade indicating a flawless coin.

MS/PR 60

Authentication Methods

Authenticating error coins is equally important as grading them. It involves verifying the coin's genuineness and ensuring that it is not a counterfeit or altered coin. Authentication is crucial in the error coin market, as some errors can be replicated or created artificially, making it essential to distinguish genuine errors from fakes.

There are several methods used to authenticate error coins. One common method is visual inspection, where experts examine the coin for any signs of tampering or alterations. They look for characteristics such as mint marks, edge reeding, and other features specific to the coin's original minting process.

Another widely used authentication method is the use of specialized equipment, such as magnification tools and electronic microscopes. These tools allow experts to examine the coin's surface in detail, looking for any signs of tampering or alterations that may not be visible to the naked eye.

In addition to visual inspection and specialized equipment, experts may also use advanced techniques such as X-ray fluorescence (XRF) analysis and spectroscopy to authenticate error coins. These methods can provide valuable information about the coin's composition and help identify any inconsistencies that may indicate tampering or counterfeiting.

Professional Grading and Authentication Services

For collectors and investors who are not experts in grading and authentication, professional grading and authentication services are available. These services employ experienced numismatists who specialize in error coins and have the necessary expertise to accurately grade and authenticate them.

Professional grading and authentication services follow strict guidelines and standards to ensure the accuracy and consistency of their assessments. They use a combination of visual inspection, specialized equipment, and advanced techniques to evaluate the condition and authenticity of error coins. Once graded and authenticated, the coins are encapsulated in tamper-evident holders, providing protection and preserving their condition.

Using professional grading and authentication services can provide peace of mind to collectors and investors, as it eliminates the risk of purchasing counterfeit or altered coins. Additionally, coins graded and authenticated by reputable services often command higher prices in the market due to the confidence and trust associated with their certification.

Chapter 2

VALUING ERROR COINS

Factors Affecting the Value of Error Coins

Type of Error: The specific type of error present on the coin significantly influences its value. Common error types include planchet errors (e.g., off-center strikes, clipped planchets), die errors (e.g., doubled dies, die cracks), and striking errors (e.g., multiple strikes, wrong metal).

Severity of Error: The severity or extent of the error plays a crucial role in determining a coin's value. More pronounced errors, such as dramatic doubling or major planchet flaws, often command higher prices due to their rarity and visual appeal.

Popularity and Demand: The popularity and demand for specific error types can greatly impact their value. Errors that are highly sought after by collectors or have gained notoriety in the numismatic community may fetch higher prices at auctions or in the secondary market.

Rarity: The rarity of an error coin is a significant determinant of its value. Rare error types or those with low survival rates are typically more desirable to collectors and command higher prices.

Condition: The overall condition or grade of the error coin also affects its value. Coins in higher grades, such as Mint State or About Uncirculated, generally command higher prices than those in lower grades due to their superior preservation and appeal.

Authentication and Certification: Coins that have been professionally authenticated and certified by reputable grading services, such as PCGS or NGC, often carry greater credibility and command higher prices in the marketplace.

Historical Significance: Some error coins gain value due to their historical significance or association with notable events or periods in numismatic history. Coins with unique or interesting backstories may attract increased interest from collectors.

Market Trends: Fluctuations in the broader coin market, as well as shifting collector preferences and trends, can impact the value of error coins. Keeping abreast of market developments and staying informed about emerging trends is essential for assessing the value of error coins accurately.

Presentation and Packaging: The presentation and packaging of an error coin can also influence its perceived value. Coins housed in attractive holders or accompanied by documentation detailing the error type and its significance may command premium prices.

Dealer Markup and Buyer Premiums: The presence of dealer markup or buyer premiums can affect the final price paid for an error coin. Understanding the pricing structure and negotiating terms with dealers or auction houses can impact the overall value proposition for collectors.

These factors collectively contribute to the value and desirability of error coins in the numismatic marketplace. Each coin is unique, and careful consideration of these factors is essential for accurately assessing its worth.

Determining the rarity of error coins

Type of Error: Some types of errors are rarer than others. For example, major die varieties like doubled dies or repunched mintmarks may be scarcer than minor errors like slight off-center strikes.

Surviving Population: The number of surviving examples of a particular error type influences its rarity. Errors that were caught during production and never released into circulation will be rarer than those that entered circulation.

Publication and Recognition:

Errors that are widely recognized and documented in numismatic literature may have established populations and known rarity levels. Conversely, newly discovered errors or those that have received limited attention may be rarer due to fewer known examples.

Collector Interest:

The level of interest from collectors can impact the perceived rarity of error coins. Errors that are highly sought after by collectors may command higher prices and appear rarer in the marketplace.

Grading and Certification: The availability of graded and certified examples can influence perceptions of rarity. Coins that have been authenticated and graded by reputable grading services may be more widely recognized and sought after by collectors.

Market Availability: The frequency with which error coins appear on the market can provide insight into their rarity. Coins that are rarely seen for sale may be considered rarer than those that are more commonly available.

Variety Within Error Types: Some error types may have variations or subtypes that affect their rarity. For example, within the category of doubled dies, there may be different degrees of doubling or variations in the affected design elements.

Condition and Quality: The condition and quality of individual specimens can affect their rarity. High-grade examples of rare error coins may be particularly scarce and command significant premiums in the marketplace.

*Expert Opinion:*Consulting with experienced numismatists, error specialists, and members of the collecting community can provide valuable insights into the rarity of specific error coins. Their knowledge and expertise can help assess factors such as population estimates and collector demand.

Pricing Guides and Resources

When it comes to collecting and investing in error coins, one of the most important aspects to consider is their value. Determining the value of an error coin can be a complex process, as it depends on various factors such as the rarity, demand, and condition of the coin. To assist collectors in this endeavor, there are several pricing guides and resources available that provide valuable insights into the market value of error coins.

Official Price Guides

Official price guides are widely recognized and trusted sources of information for determining the value of error coins. These guides are often published by reputable organizations and provide comprehensive listings of various error coin types along with their corresponding market values. Some of the most popular official price guides include:

- **The Official Red Book**: Published annually by Whitman Publishing, The Official Red Book is considered the definitive guide for U.S. coin values. It includes a section dedicated to error coins, providing detailed information on their rarity and estimated values.
- **The Blue Book**: Also published by Whitman Publishing, The Blue Book is another widely used

reference guide for U.S. coin values. While it doesn't focus specifically on error coins, it provides a general overview of coin values, which can be helpful in determining the baseline value of an error coin.

- **The PCGS Price Guide**: The Professional Coin Grading Service (PCGS) is a highly respected coin grading and authentication company. They offer an online price guide that provides up-to-date market values for various error coins. The PCGS Price Guide is known for its accuracy and is frequently used by collectors and dealers alike.

Online Resources

In addition to official price guides, there are numerous online resources available that can assist collectors in determining the value of their error coins. These resources often provide real-time market data, auction results, and price trends, allowing collectors to stay informed about the current value of their coins. Some popular online resources include:

- **Coin Auction Websites**: Websites such as eBay, Heritage Auctions, and Stack's Bowers Galleries regularly host coin auctions where error coins are bought and sold. These auction platforms can provide valuable insights into the market value of specific error coin varieties.

- **Coin Forums and Communities**: Online coin forums and communities are excellent resources for collectors to connect with fellow enthusiasts and gain knowledge about error coins. These platforms often have dedicated sections where collectors can discuss pricing trends, share their experiences, and seek advice on valuing their error coins.

- **Coin Price Aggregator Websites**: There are several websites that aggregate coin prices from various sources, providing collectors with a comprehensive overview of the market value of error coins. These websites often include price charts, historical data, and price analysis tools to help collectors make informed decisions about their collections.

Coin Shows and Conventions

Attending coin shows and conventions can be a great way to gain firsthand knowledge about the value of error coins. These events bring together collectors, dealers, and experts from around the world, creating a vibrant marketplace for buying, selling, and trading coins. Coin shows often feature educational seminars and workshops where experts share their insights on error coin pricing and market trends. Additionally, collectors can interact with dealers and experts directly, gaining valuable advice and guidance on valuing their error coins.

Professional Coin Dealers and Appraisers

For collectors who prefer a more personalized approach, consulting with professional coin dealers and appraisers can be highly beneficial. These experts have extensive knowledge and experience in the field of error coins and can provide accurate assessments of their value. Professional coin dealers and appraisers stay up-to-date with the latest market trends and have access to pricing databases and resources that may not be readily available to the general public. They can also provide guidance on the best strategies for buying, selling, and investing in error coins.

It is important to note that while pricing guides and resources can provide valuable insights into the value of error coins, the market for these coins can be highly subjective and influenced by various factors. Collectors should use these resources as a starting point and consider additional factors such as the condition, rarity, and demand for a particular error coin when determining its value. Regularly staying informed about market trends and consulting with experts can help collectors make informed decisions and maximize the potential profit from their error coin collections.

Remember, the value of error coins can fluctuate over time, so it is essential to stay updated with the latest pricing information and market trends to make informed decisions about buying, selling, and investing in these unique and fascinating coins.

Market Trends and Demand for Error Coins

As a collector of error coins, it is important to stay informed about the market trends and demand for these unique and valuable pieces. Understanding the current state of the market can help you make informed decisions about buying, selling, and investing in error coins. In this section, we will explore the market trends and demand for error coins in 2024.

The Growing Popularity of Error Coins

Over the past few years, the popularity of error coins has been steadily increasing. More and more collectors are recognizing the unique appeal and investment potential of these coins. This growing interest has led to an increase in demand for error coins, driving up their prices in the market.

One of the reasons for the rising popularity of error coins is the thrill of the hunt. Collectors enjoy the challenge of searching for these rare and elusive coins, whether it's through pocket change, bank rolls, or specialized coin dealers. The excitement of finding an error coin adds an element of adventure to the hobby, making it even more appealing to collectors.

Additionally, the internet has played a significant role in the increased popularity of error coins. Online platforms and forums dedicated to coin collecting have made it easier for collectors to connect, share information, and buy/sell error coins. This accessibility has helped create a vibrant and active community of error coin enthusiasts, further fueling the demand for these unique pieces.

Factors Influencing the Market Trends

Several factors influence the market trends and demand for error coins. Understanding these factors can help collectors make informed decisions about their collections.

Rarity and Scarcity

The rarity and scarcity of an error coin play a significant role in determining its value and demand. Coins with unique and highly visible errors are generally more sought after by collectors. The rarer the error, the higher the demand and price. As a collector, it is important to stay updated on the latest discoveries and research regarding rare error coins to identify potential investment opportunities.

Condition and Grade

The condition and grade of an error coin also impact its market value. Well-preserved coins with minimal wear and damage are generally more desirable to collectors. Grading services play a crucial role in determining the condition and authenticity of error coins. Coins that have been professionally graded and authenticated tend to command higher prices in the market.

Popular Coin Series

Certain coin series have a dedicated following of collectors who actively seek out error coins within those series. For example, the Lincoln cent series is known for its numerous error varieties, making it a popular choice among error coin collectors. The demand for error coins within popular series remains consistently high, driving up their market value.

Investing in Error Coins

In addition to collecting for personal enjoyment, many collectors also view error coins as an investment opportunity. The market trends and demand for error coins make them an attractive option for those looking to diversify their investment portfolios. However, it is important to approach error coin investing with caution and a thorough understanding of the market.

When investing in error coins, it is crucial to research and identify coins with strong potential for future appreciation. This involves staying updated on the latest market trends, understanding the factors that drive demand, and seeking expert advice when necessary. It is also important to consider the long-term outlook for error coins as an investment and to have a well-defined investment strategy in place.

The Future of the Error Coin Market

The future of the error coin market looks promising. As more collectors enter the hobby and the demand for error coins continues to grow, the market is expected to remain strong. Advancements in technology and increased accessibility to information will likely contribute to the continued popularity of error coins.

However, it is important to note that the market for error coins can be subject to fluctuations. Like any investment, there are risks involved, and prices can go up or down depending on various factors. Therefore, it is essential for collectors and investors to stay informed, conduct thorough research, and make informed decisions based on their individual goals and risk tolerance.

In conclusion, the market trends and demand for error coins are on the rise. The growing popularity of these unique and valuable coins, coupled with factors such as rarity, condition, historical significance, and the appeal of popular coin series, contribute to their increasing market value. Whether you collect error coins for personal enjoyment or as an investment, staying informed about the market trends and demand is crucial for making informed decisions and maximizing the potential of your collection.

Appraising and Selling Error Coins

Once you have built a collection of rare error coins, it's important to understand how to appraise and sell them effectively. Appraising error coins involves determining their value based on various factors such as rarity, condition, demand, and market trends. Selling error coins requires careful consideration of the best platforms and strategies to maximize your profits. In this section, we will explore the process of appraising and selling error coins, providing you with valuable insights and tips to navigate the market successfully.

Appraising Error Coins

Appraising error coins is a crucial step in understanding their value and potential profitability. Several factors contribute to the appraisal process, including the rarity of the error, the demand for that particular type of error, the condition of the coin, and the overall market trends. Here are some key steps to follow when appraising your error coins:

1. ***Research and Education****:* Before appraising your error coins, it's essential to educate yourself about the different types of errors, their rarity, and the current market conditions. Stay updated with pricing guides, auction results, and online forums to gain a comprehensive understanding of the value of your error coins.

2. ***Consult Experts****:* Seek advice from experienced numismatists or professional coin appraisers who specialize in error coins. Their expertise can provide valuable insights into the rarity and value of your specific error coins. They can also help authenticate your coins and provide grading opinions, which can significantly impact their value.

3. ***Compare Similar Sales****:* Look for recent sales of similar error coins to get an idea of their market value. Online auction platforms, coin shows, and specialized error coin dealers are excellent sources for comparing prices. Consider the condition and rarity of your coins when comparing sales to determine a fair appraisal.

4. ***Consider Grading****:* The condition of your error coins plays a significant role in their value. Consider having your coins professionally graded by reputable grading services such as PCGS or NGC. Grading provides an unbiased assessment of

the coin's condition, which can help determine its value more accurately.

5. ***Document and Preserve:*** Keep detailed records of your error coins, including their type, date, mintmark, condition, and any relevant information. Properly store and preserve your coins in protective holders or albums to maintain their condition and enhance their value.

Selling Error Coins

Once you have appraised your error coins, it's time to consider selling them. Selling error coins can be a rewarding experience, both financially and for the satisfaction of sharing your collection with other enthusiasts. Here are some strategies to help you sell your error coins effectively:

1. ***Choose the Right Platform:*** Selecting the right platform to sell your error coins is crucial. Consider online auction platforms such as eBay or specialized numismatic websites that cater to error coin collectors. These platforms provide a wide reach and attract potential buyers specifically interested in error coins.

2. ***Set a Competitive Price:*** Price your error coins competitively based on their appraised value and market demand. Consider starting with a slightly

higher price to allow room for negotiation. Providing detailed descriptions and high-quality images of your coins can attract potential buyers and justify your asking price.

3. *Market Your Coins:* Utilize various marketing strategies to promote your error coins effectively. Create compelling listings with accurate descriptions, highlighting the unique features and rarity of your coins. Utilize social media platforms, online forums, and numismatic communities to reach potential buyers who share your passion for error coins.

4. *Consider Consignment:* If you prefer not to sell your error coins directly, consider consigning them to reputable coin dealers or auction houses. Consignment allows you to leverage their established customer base and expertise in selling rare coins. However, be aware that consignment fees and commissions may apply.

5. *Attend Coin Shows:* Coin shows provide an excellent opportunity to showcase and sell your error coins directly to collectors and dealers. Research local and national coin shows and consider setting up a booth or table to display your collection. Engage with potential buyers, share your knowledge, and build connections within the numismatic community.

6. ***Be Patient****:* Selling error coins may take time, especially if you are looking for the right buyer who appreciates the rarity and value of your collection. Be patient and persistent in your efforts, and consider adjusting your pricing or marketing strategies if necessary.

Remember, the value of error coins can fluctuate over time, so it's essential to stay informed about market trends and adjust your selling strategies accordingly. By following these tips and staying actively engaged in the numismatic community, you can maximize your profits and ensure a successful selling experience.

Investing in Error Coins

Investing in error coins can be a lucrative and exciting venture for collectors and investors alike. While the primary motivation for collecting error coins is often the love of the hobby, it is important to understand the potential financial benefits that can come from investing in these unique and valuable pieces. In this section, we will explore the various aspects of investing in error coins, including the potential for profit, strategies for building a profitable portfolio, and the risks involved.

The Potential for Profit

Investing in error coins can offer significant profit potential for those who are knowledgeable and strategic in their approach. The rarity and uniqueness of error coins often make them highly sought after by collectors, which can drive up their value over time. Additionally, the growing interest in error coins among both seasoned collectors and new enthusiasts can contribute to increased demand and higher prices.

One of the key factors that can influence the potential for profit is the rarity of the error coin. The scarcer the error, the more valuable it is likely to be. As a collector and investor, it is important to stay informed about the market trends and demand for different types of error coins. This knowledge can help you identify the most valuable and potentially profitable pieces to add to your collection.

Another important consideration when investing in error coins is the condition or grade of the coin. Higher-grade error coins generally command higher prices, as they are more visually appealing and desirable to collectors. Therefore, it is essential to learn about the grading and authentication process to accurately assess the value of the coins you are considering for investment.

Building a Profitable Portfolio

Building a profitable portfolio of error coins requires careful planning and research. Here are some strategies to consider:

1. ***Diversify Your Collection:*** Just like with any investment, diversification is key. By acquiring error coins from different categories and time periods, you can spread your risk and increase the potential for profit. Consider investing in a variety of error types, such as off-center strikes, double dies, clipped planchets, and broadstrikes.

2. ***Focus on Rarity***: As mentioned earlier, rarity plays a significant role in the value of error coins. Look for error coins that are scarce or have unique characteristics that make them stand out from the rest. These coins are more likely to appreciate in value over time.

3. ***Stay Informed:*** Keep up with the latest market trends and developments in the error coin collecting community. Join online forums, attend coin shows, and read books and articles to stay informed about new discoveries, pricing trends, and collector preferences. This knowledge will help you make informed investment decisions.

4. ***Consider Professional Grading:*** Having your error coins professionally graded and authenticated can

add credibility and value to your collection. Third-party grading services provide unbiased assessments of the condition and authenticity of your coins, which can be crucial when it comes to selling or trading them in the future.

5. ***Long-Term Perspective:*** Investing in error coins should be viewed as a long-term endeavor. While some coins may appreciate quickly, others may take years to reach their full potential. Patience and a long-term perspective are essential for maximizing your investment returns.

Risks and Considerations

As with any investment, there are risks involved in investing in error coins. It is important to be aware of these risks and take them into account when making investment decisions. Here are some key considerations:

1. ***Market Volatility:*** The market for error coins can be volatile, with prices fluctuating based on collector demand, market conditions, and other factors. Prices can rise and fall rapidly, so it is important to be prepared for potential fluctuations in the value of your investment.

2. ***Counterfeits and Altered Coins:*** The risk of encountering counterfeit or altered error coins is a concern in the numismatic world. It is crucial to

educate yourself about the characteristics and diagnostics of genuine error coins to avoid falling victim to fraudulent pieces. Buying from reputable dealers and having coins professionally authenticated can help mitigate this risk.

3. ***Storage and Security:*** Proper storage and security are essential for protecting your investment. Error coins should be stored in a secure and controlled environment to prevent damage, theft, or loss. Consider investing in high-quality coin holders, safes, or safety deposit boxes to ensure the long-term preservation of your collection.

4. ***Liquidity:*** While error coins can be highly valuable, they may not always be easy to sell quickly. The market for error coins can be relatively niche, and finding the right buyer at the right time may require patience. It is important to have a realistic understanding of the potential liquidity of your investment.

Chapter 3

BUILDING A COLLECTION

Setting Collecting Goals

Setting clear collecting goals is an essential step in building a successful and fulfilling error coin collection. By defining your objectives, you can focus your efforts, make informed decisions, and ultimately achieve the desired outcomes. In this section, we will explore the importance of setting collecting goals and provide guidance on how to establish them effectively.

Understanding the Purpose of Collecting Goals

Before diving into the specifics of setting collecting goals, it is crucial to understand why they are essential. Collecting goals serve as a roadmap for your collection, guiding your choices and actions. They provide direction, motivation, and a sense of purpose. By establishing clear objectives, you can make informed decisions about which error coins to pursue, how to allocate your resources, and when to make additions or adjustments to your collection.

Defining Your Collecting Objectives

To begin setting your collecting goals, take some time to reflect on what you hope to achieve with your error coin collection. Consider the following questions:

1. What is your primary motivation for collecting error coins? Are you interested in the historical significance, the thrill of the hunt, or the potential for financial gain?
2. Are you aiming to build a comprehensive collection that covers a wide range of error coin varieties, or do you prefer to specialize in specific types or time periods?
3. Do you plan to collect error coins for personal enjoyment, or do you also have aspirations to profit from your collection in the future?
4. Are you interested in acquiring error coins solely for their numismatic value, or do you also appreciate the aesthetic appeal of these unique pieces?

By answering these questions, you can gain clarity on your collecting objectives and tailor your approach accordingly.

Setting Realistic and Achievable Goals

While it is important to dream big, it is equally crucial to set realistic and achievable goals for your error coin collection. Consider the following factors when establishing your objectives:

1. Budget: Assess your financial resources and determine how much you are willing and able to invest in your collection. Setting a realistic budget will help you make informed decisions about which error coins to pursue and how to allocate your funds effectively.

2. Time Commitment: Consider the amount of time you can dedicate to your collecting endeavors. Collecting error coins can be a time-consuming hobby, especially if you are actively searching for them in circulation or attending coin shows and auctions. Set goals that align with your available time and energy.

3. Knowledge and Expertise: Be honest about your level of knowledge and expertise in the field of error coin collecting. If you are a beginner, it may be more realistic to start with a narrower focus and gradually expand your collection as you gain experience and understanding.

4. Space and Storage: Evaluate the physical space available for your collection and consider the

storage options that best suit your needs. Setting goals that align with your storage capabilities will help you avoid clutter and ensure the proper preservation of your error coins.

Documenting and Reviewing Your Goals

Once you have defined your collecting goals, it is essential to document them in a clear and organized manner. Create a written record of your objectives, including specific details such as the types of error coins you wish to collect, any specific time periods or denominations you are interested in, and any financial or time constraints you have set for yourself.

Regularly review and reassess your goals to ensure they remain relevant and aligned with your evolving interests and circumstances. As you gain more knowledge and experience in error coin collecting, you may find it necessary to adjust or expand your objectives. By regularly reviewing your goals, you can stay focused and motivated on your collecting journey.

Seeking Guidance and Inspiration

Setting collecting goals can be an exciting and personal process, but it can also be helpful to seek guidance and inspiration from experienced collectors and numismatic experts. Joining online forums, attending coin club meetings, and engaging with the error coin collecting community can provide valuable insights and perspectives. Learn from the experiences of others and use their expertise to refine and enhance your own collecting goals.

Remember, collecting error coins is a journey, and your goals may evolve and change over time. Embrace the process, stay open to new opportunities, and enjoy the thrill of building a unique and valuable error coin collection.

Creating a Budget for Collecting Error Coins

When it comes to collecting error coins, one of the most important aspects to consider is creating a budget. Having a well-planned budget will not only help you stay organized but also ensure that you can acquire the coins you desire without overspending. In this section, we will discuss the key factors to consider when creating a budget for collecting error coins.

Assessing Your Financial Situation

Before diving into the world of error coin collecting, it is crucial to assess your financial situation. Take a close look at your income, expenses, and any other financial obligations you may have. Understanding your financial standing will help you determine how much you can comfortably allocate towards your coin collecting hobby.

Consider your disposable income, which is the amount of money you have left after covering all your necessary expenses. It is important to be realistic and set aside a portion of your disposable income for error coin collecting. Remember, collecting error coins should be an enjoyable hobby, not a financial burden.

Setting a Realistic Budget

Once you have assessed your financial situation, it is time to set a realistic budget for your error coin collecting endeavors. Start by determining how much you can comfortably allocate towards your collection on a monthly or yearly basis. This will depend on your disposable income and other financial commitments.

When setting your budget, it is important to strike a balance between acquiring new error coins and managing your overall finances. Avoid overspending or stretching your budget too thin, as this can lead to financial stress and potentially hinder your ability to enjoy your collection.

Researching Coin Prices and Market Trends

To create an effective budget, it is essential to research coin prices and stay updated on market trends. Understanding the current market value of error coins will help you make informed decisions when allocating your budget.

Utilize pricing guides, online resources, and reputable coin dealers to gather information on the value of different error coin varieties. Keep in mind that prices can fluctuate over time, so it is important to stay up-to-date with the latest market trends. This will enable you to make educated decisions when purchasing error coins and ensure that you are getting the best value for your budget.

Prioritizing Your Collecting Goals

When working with a budget, it is important to prioritize your collecting goals. Determine which error coin varieties or specific coins you are most interested in acquiring. This will help you allocate your budget towards the coins that align with your collecting objectives.

Consider creating a list of your top priorities and allocate a portion of your budget specifically for those coins. This will ensure that you are actively working towards your collecting goals while staying within your financial means. As you achieve your goals, you can reassess and adjust your budget accordingly.

Allotting Funds for Unexpected Opportunities

While it is important to have a well-planned budget, it is also wise to set aside a portion of your funds for unexpected opportunities. In the world of error coin collecting, unique and rare coins can sometimes become available at short notice. Having a reserve fund will allow you to take advantage of these opportunities without disrupting your overall budget.

Consider allocating a small percentage of your budget towards these unexpected opportunities. This will give you the flexibility to seize rare error coins that may not have been part of your initial collecting plan. However, it is important to exercise caution and ensure that these impromptu purchases align with your overall collecting goals and budget.

Tracking and Evaluating Your Spending

Once you have established a budget, it is crucial to track and evaluate your spending regularly. Keep a record of your purchases, including the cost of each error coin and any associated expenses such as shipping or authentication fees. This will help you stay accountable and ensure that you are staying within your budgetary limits.

Regularly evaluate your spending patterns and assess whether adjustments need to be made. If you find that you are consistently overspending or struggling to stay within your budget, consider reevaluating your collecting goals or adjusting your budget accordingly. Remember, the key is to enjoy your collection while maintaining financial stability.

Seeking Professional Advice

If you are new to error coin collecting or find it challenging to create a budget, consider seeking professional advice. Consult with experienced collectors, numismatic experts, or financial advisors who can provide guidance on creating a budget that suits your specific needs and goals.

Professional advice can help you navigate the complexities of error coin collecting and ensure that you are making informed decisions with your budget. They can provide insights into market trends, pricing strategies, and help you optimize your collecting experience.

Building a Diverse Error Coin Collection

Building a diverse error coin collection is an exciting and rewarding endeavor. By acquiring a wide range of error coin varieties, you can showcase the unique and fascinating aspects of this niche within the coin collecting world. In this section, we will explore the strategies and considerations for building a diverse error coin collection that will captivate both seasoned collectors and newcomers to the hobby.

Setting Collecting Goals

Before embarking on your journey to build a diverse error coin collection, it is essential to establish your collecting goals. Consider what aspects of error coins intrigue you the most. Are you interested in a specific type of error, such as double dies or off-center strikes? Or do you prefer to collect a variety of error coin types to showcase the breadth of this fascinating field?

Setting collecting goals will help you focus your efforts and guide your decision-making process. It will also provide a sense of direction and purpose as you navigate the vast world of error coins. Whether you aim to build a comprehensive collection or focus on a specific error coin variety, having clear goals will enhance your collecting experience.

Creating a Budget for Collecting Error Coins

Like any collecting hobby, error coin collecting requires careful financial planning. Before diving into the world of error coins, it is crucial to establish a budget that aligns with your collecting goals. Determine how much you are willing to invest in your collection and allocate funds accordingly.

When creating a budget, consider the rarity and desirability of the error coins you wish to acquire. Some error coins may command higher prices due to their scarcity or historical significance. It is essential to strike a balance between your collecting goals and your financial capabilities.

Additionally, keep in mind that error coin prices can fluctuate over time. Stay informed about market trends and consult pricing guides and resources to ensure that your budget remains realistic and up-to-date.

Building a Diverse Error Coin Collection

Building a diverse error coin collection involves acquiring a wide range of error coin varieties. By diversifying your collection, you can showcase the different types of errors and their unique characteristics. Here are some strategies to consider when building a diverse error coin collection:

Exploring Different Error Coin Types

One way to diversify your collection is by exploring different error coin types. Error coins come in various forms, including double dies, off-center strikes, clipped planchets, and broadstrikes, among others. Each type offers its own distinct appeal and collecting challenges.

By acquiring error coins from different types, you can appreciate the nuances and variations within the error coin realm. It also allows you to showcase the breadth of your collection and engage with fellow collectors who may have a specific interest in a particular error coin type.

Seeking Different Denominations and Minting Years

Another strategy for building a diverse error coin collection is to seek error coins from different denominations and minting years. Error coins can be found in various denominations, including pennies, nickels, dimes, quarters, and dollars. Each denomination presents its own set of error possibilities, making it an exciting endeavor to collect error coins across different coin types.

Furthermore, exploring error coins from different minting years adds depth and historical significance to your collection. By acquiring error coins from various years, you can trace the evolution of minting processes and appreciate the unique errors that occurred during specific time periods.

Collecting Error Coins from Different Countries

Error coins are not limited to a specific country or region. They can be found in coins from all around the world. Collecting error coins from different countries adds an international flair to your collection and allows you to explore the rich diversity of error coins globally.

By acquiring error coins from different countries, you can learn about their unique minting processes, error types, and historical contexts. It also provides an opportunity to connect with collectors from different parts of the world and exchange knowledge and experiences.

Organizing and Displaying Your Collection

Once you have built a diverse error coin collection, it is essential to organize and display your coins effectively. Proper organization ensures that you can easily access and appreciate your collection, while thoughtful display methods allow you to showcase your coins to their fullest potential.

Consider using coin albums, folders, or display cases specifically designed for error coins. These storage options provide protection from environmental factors and allow you to arrange your coins in a visually appealing manner. Labeling and cataloging your coins will also help you keep track of your collection and its unique attributes.

When displaying your collection, consider factors such as lighting, security, and accessibility. Displaying your error coins in a well-lit area with proper security measures will enhance their visual appeal and protect them from potential damage or theft. Additionally, consider sharing your collection with fellow collectors through online platforms or local coin clubs to foster a sense of community and appreciation for error coins.

Building a diverse error coin collection requires patience, research, and a passion for the hobby. By setting collecting goals, creating a budget, and exploring different error coin types, denominations, minting years, and countries, you can build a collection that reflects your unique interests and captivates the attention of fellow collectors. Remember to organize and display your collection with care, allowing your error coins to shine and tell their fascinating stories.

Organizing and Displaying Your Collection

Once you have started building your collection of rare error coins, it is important to have a system in place for organizing and displaying your treasures. Proper organization not only allows you to easily access and enjoy your collection, but it also helps you keep track of what you have and identify any gaps in your collection. Additionally, a well-displayed collection can be a source of pride and a great conversation starter for fellow coin enthusiasts. In this section, we will explore some tips and techniques for organizing and displaying your error coin collection.

Choosing the Right Storage Solution

The first step in organizing your collection is to choose the right storage solution. There are several options available, each with its own advantages and considerations. A few popular storage options will be discussed in next chapter.

Organizing Your Collection

Once you have chosen the right storage solution for your error coins, it's time to organize your collection. The organization method you choose will depend on your personal preferences and the size of your collection. Here are a few popular ways to organize error coin collections:

1. ***By Date and Mint Mark****:* Organizing your error coins by date and mint mark is a common method used by collectors. This method allows you to easily track the progression of errors over time and identify any gaps in your collection. You can use coin albums or coin holders with labeled dividers to separate your coins by year and mint mark.

2. ***By Error Type****:* Another popular method of organization is grouping your error coins by type. For example, you can create sections for off-center strikes, double dies, clipped planchets, and other error varieties. This method allows you to compare and study different error types more easily.

3. ***By Rarity or Value****:* If you are primarily interested in the rarity or value of your error coins, you may choose to organize your collection based on these factors. You can create sections for rare or valuable error coins and separate them from more common varieties. This method can help you quickly identify the most valuable coins in your collection.

4. ***By Theme or Design****:* For collectors who appreciate the aesthetics of error coins, organizing by theme or design can be a visually appealing option. You can group coins with similar themes or

designs together, creating a cohesive and visually striking display.

How to Display Your Collection

Once your error coin collection is organized, it's time to display it in a way that showcases its beauty and uniqueness.

Coin Frames: Coin frames are an excellent way to display individual error coins or small sets. These frames typically consist of a clear plastic or glass cover that holds the coin in place. Coin frames can be hung on the wall or displayed on a shelf, allowing you to enjoy your coins while keeping them protected.

Shadow Boxes: Shadow boxes are deep, framed display cases that can hold multiple coins or sets. They provide a three-dimensional display and allow you to arrange your coins in a visually appealing manner. Shadow boxes are a great option for creating themed displays or showcasing a specific series of error coins.

Display Stands: Display stands are a simple and affordable way to showcase individual error coins. These stands typically consist of a small, clear plastic base that holds the coin upright. Display stands are ideal for highlighting specific coins or rotating your display periodically.

Glass Display Cases: If you have a larger collection or want to protect your coins from dust and handling, glass display cases are a great option. These cases come in various sizes and can be customized with shelves or compartments to accommodate your collection. Glass display cases provide a secure and elegant way to showcase your error coins.

Try to keep your displayed collection away from direct sunlight, extreme temperatures, and high humidity to prevent damage to your coins. Regularly dusting and cleaning your display area will help keep your collection looking its best.

Chapter 4

SPECIALIZED ERROR COIN VARIETIES

Off-Center Strikes

Off-center strikes are one of the most fascinating and sought-after types of error coins. These coins are the result of a misalignment during the minting process, causing the design to be struck off-center on the coin's surface. The degree of off-centering can vary, ranging from minor to extreme, and can greatly affect the value and desirability of the coin.

Off-center strikes can be identified by several distinct characteristics. The most obvious is the misalignment of the design elements on the coin. Instead of being centered, the design will appear shifted towards one side, leaving a blank or partially blank area on the opposite side. The degree of off-centering can vary, with some coins showing only a slight shift, while others may have the design completely off the coin's surface.

Another characteristic to look for is the presence of a raised rim on one side of the coin. This occurs because the metal is forced towards the opposite side during the striking process, causing the metal to flow and form a raised rim. The size and shape of the raised rim can vary depending on the degree of off-centering.

Additionally, off-center strikes often exhibit a distorted or elongated design. This is due to the pressure exerted on the metal during the striking process, causing the design elements to stretch or compress in the direction of the off-center strike.

Rarity and Value of Off-Center Strikes

The rarity and value of off-center strikes depend on several factors, including the degree of off-centering, the type of coin, and the demand from collectors. Generally, the more off-center the strike, the rarer and more valuable the coin becomes.

Coins with minor off-center strikes, where only a small portion of the design is affected, are more common and generally have lower values. These coins are still interesting to collectors but may not command a significant premium.

On the other hand, coins with extreme off-center strikes, where a large portion or the entire design is off the coin's surface, are highly sought after by collectors. These coins are much rarer and can command substantial premiums in the market.

The type of coin also plays a role in determining the value of off-center strikes. Coins with high collector demand, such as rare or key date coins, will generally have higher values when affected by an off-center strike. Additionally, off-center strikes on popular coin series or denominations may also attract more attention from collectors, further increasing their value.

Collecting and Profiting from Off-Center Strikes

Collecting off-center strikes can be an exciting and rewarding endeavor. Not only do these coins offer a unique and visually appealing aspect to any collection, but they also have the potential for significant appreciation in value over time.

To start collecting off-center strikes, it is essential to educate yourself on the various types of coins and their off-centering tendencies. Some coin series or denominations may be more prone to off-center strikes than others, so focusing on those areas can increase your chances of finding these unique coins.

One of the best ways to acquire off-center strikes is through coin dealers, online marketplaces, or coin shows. These sources often have a wide selection of error coins, including off-center strikes, and can provide valuable guidance and expertise in building your collection.

When purchasing off-center strikes, it is crucial to consider the degree of off-centering, the condition of the coin, and its overall appeal to collectors. Coins with more extreme off-center strikes and minimal damage or wear will generally command higher prices.

As with any investment, it is important to keep in mind that the value of off-center strikes can fluctuate over time. Market demand, collector trends, and the overall condition of the coin can all impact its value. Therefore, it is advisable to stay informed about the market and regularly assess the value of your collection.

Double Dies

One of the most fascinating and sought-after types of error coins is the double die. A double die occurs when there is a mechanical error during the minting process that causes the design or lettering on a coin to be struck more than once, resulting in a doubled image. This creates a unique and visually striking effect that collectors find highly desirable.

What Causes Double Dies?

Double dies occur when the coin dies, which are used to strike the design onto the coin blanks, are not properly aligned during the minting process. This misalignment causes the design elements to be struck twice, resulting in a doubling effect. The most common cause of double dies is a misalignment of the hub and the working die, which can happen due to various factors such as worn-out or misaligned machinery, improper maintenance, or human error.

Identifying Double Dies

Identifying a double die can be an exciting and rewarding experience for collectors. The most obvious sign of a double die is the presence of doubling in the design or lettering on the coin. This doubling can be seen as a shadow or a ghost-like image that appears slightly offset from the original design. The doubling is usually most noticeable on the inscriptions, date, or mint mark of the coin.

To identify a double die, it is important to carefully examine the coin under proper lighting conditions. Using a magnifying glass or a loupe can also help in detecting the doubling more clearly. It is essential to compare the coin with a regular version of the same coin to confirm the presence of a double die.

Repunched Mint Mark Error

A repunched mint mark error occurs when the mint mark is punched onto the die more than once, resulting in a mint mark that appears doubled or tripled. This error is most commonly found on coins that have a mint mark, such as the "D" for Denver or "S" for San Francisco. Repunched mint mark errors can add value to a coin, especially if the doubling is prominent.

Notable Double Die Varieties

Over the years, there have been several notable double die varieties that have captured the attention of collectors.

One of the most famous examples is the 1955 Lincoln Cent double die, also known as the "Doubled Die Obverse" or DDO. This coin features a prominent doubling of the date and the inscriptions "LIBERTY" and "IN GOD WE TRUST." The 1955 DDO is highly sought after and commands a significant premium in the market.

Another notable double die variety is the 1969-S Lincoln Cent double die, also known as the "Doubled Die

Obverse" or DDO. This coin exhibits doubling on the date and the inscriptions "LIBERTY" and "IN GOD WE TRUST." The 1969-S DDO is considered one of the most valuable and rare double dies in the Lincoln Cent series.

Apart from these famous examples, there are numerous other double die varieties across different denominations and coin series. Some other notable double dies include the 1943-P Jefferson Nickel double die, the 1983-P Washington Quarter double die, and the 2004-D Wisconsin State Quarter double die.

Collecting and Valuing Double Dies

Collecting double dies can be an exciting and rewarding endeavor for coin enthusiasts. The rarity and visual appeal of these error coins make them highly sought after by collectors. The value of a double die coin is determined by several factors, including its rarity, demand, condition, and the overall appeal of the doubling effect.

To determine the value of a double die coin, collectors often refer to pricing guides, online resources, and consult with experienced collectors or professional coin dealers. It is important to note that the value of a double die can vary significantly depending on its rarity and the demand in the market. Some double dies may command a premium of several hundred or even thousands of dollars, while others may have a more modest value.

When collecting double dies, it is essential to consider the condition of the coin. Like any other collectible coin, the value of a double die can be greatly affected by its condition. Coins in higher grades, such as Mint State or Proof, are generally more desirable and command higher prices in the market.

Authenticating Double Dies

Authenticating a double die coin is crucial to ensure its value and legitimacy. Due to the popularity and value of double dies, there have been instances of counterfeit or altered coins being passed off as genuine double dies. To authenticate a double die, it is recommended to seek the expertise of professional coin grading and authentication services.

These services employ advanced techniques and equipment to examine the coin and determine its authenticity. They also provide a certification or encapsulation that guarantees the coin's authenticity and grade. Collectors should always purchase double dies from reputable sources and ensure that the coin has been authenticated by a trusted third-party service.

Clipped Planchets

One of the fascinating and sought-after error coin varieties is the clipped planchet. A clipped planchet occurs when a portion of the coin's blank is missing due to an error during the minting process. This error can result in a unique and visually striking coin that collectors eagerly seek to add to their collections.

A clipped planchet error occurs when a blank coin disc, also known as a planchet, is improperly cut during the minting process. This can happen when the cutting machine malfunctions or when the metal strip used to produce the planchets is misaligned. As a result, a portion of the planchet is missing, creating an irregular shape on the finished coin.

The clipped area on the coin can vary in size and location. It can be a small clip, known as a "minor clip," where only a small portion of the coin is missing. Alternatively, it can be a larger clip, known as a "major clip," where a significant portion of the coin's circumference is absent. The shape of the clipped area can range from a straight edge to a curved or irregular shape, depending on the angle at which the planchet was cut.

Types of Clipped Planchets

Clipped planchets can be classified into different types based on the location and size of the clipped area. The most common types include:

1. Straight Clip: This type of clipped planchet occurs when a portion of the coin's edge is missing in a straight line. It can be a minor or major straight clip, depending on the size of the missing metal.
2. Curved Clip: A curved clip happens when a portion of the coin's edge is missing in a curved or semi-circular shape. This type of clipped planchet can create visually appealing coins with unique shapes.
3. Ragged Clip: A ragged clip occurs when the missing portion of the coin's edge has an irregular or jagged shape. This type of clipped planchet can result from a misaligned cutting machine or other mechanical issues during the minting process.
4. Elliptical Clip: An elliptical clip is characterized by a missing portion of the coin's edge in an elliptical or oval shape. This type of clipped planchet can

create coins with an interesting and distinctive appearance.

Rarity and Value of Clipped Planchets

The rarity and value of clipped planchets can vary depending on several factors, including the size, location, and overall visual appeal of the error. Generally, major clips are more desirable and valuable than minor clips due to their larger missing portions. Coins with unique or unusual shapes, such as curved or ragged clips, are also highly sought after by collectors.

The value of a clipped planchet error coin is also influenced by its condition and grade. Coins with minimal wear and damage are typically more valuable than those with significant signs of circulation or damage. Additionally, the rarity of the specific coin design and year can also impact its value.

To determine the value of a clipped planchet error coin, collectors often refer to pricing guides, consult with experienced numismatists, or browse online auction platforms to see recent sales of similar coins. It's important to note that the value of error coins can fluctuate over time due to market demand and availability.

Collecting and Profiting from Clipped Planchets

Collecting clipped planchet error coins can be an exciting and rewarding endeavor. These unique coins add diversity and intrigue to any collection. Here are some tips for collecting and potentially profiting from clipped planchet error coins:

1. Research and Education: Familiarize yourself with the different types of clipped planchets and their characteristics. Study reference materials, online resources, and join numismatic communities to enhance your knowledge.
2. Quality and Condition: Aim to acquire clipped planchet error coins in the best possible condition. Coins with minimal wear and damage will generally command higher prices in the collector's market.
3. Variety and Rarity: Look for coins with unusual or rare clipped planchet errors. Coins with distinctive shapes or larger missing portions are often more desirable among collectors.
4. Authentication and Certification: Consider having your clipped planchet error coins authenticated and certified by a reputable third-party grading service. This can enhance the coin's marketability and value.

5. Networking and Selling: Connect with other collectors, attend coin shows, and explore online platforms to buy, sell, or trade clipped planchet error coins. Building relationships within the numismatic community can provide opportunities to acquire rare specimens and potentially profit from your collection.

See, collecting error coins, including clipped planchets, as a long-term investment. It requires patience, research, and a passion for the hobby. Enjoy the journey of discovering these unique and valuable coins, and may your collection continue to grow in both knowledge and value.

Broadstrikes and Brockages

Broadstrikes and brockages are two fascinating and highly sought-after error coin varieties that can add significant value and intrigue to any collection. In this section, we will explore the characteristics, rarity, and market demand for these unique error coins, as well as provide tips on how to identify and profit from them.

Broadstrikes

Broadstrikes are error coins that occur when a coin is struck without the collar, resulting in a coin that lacks the usual reeded edge. Instead, the metal expands outward, creating a broad and flat appearance. This error can occur in both the obverse and reverse sides of the coin, and the absence of the collar allows the design to spread beyond the intended boundaries.

Identifying a broadstrike error coin is relatively straightforward. Look for coins that lack the reeded edge and have a larger diameter than normal. The absence of the collar may also cause the design to appear distorted or elongated. Additionally, broadstrikes often exhibit a concave shape due to the metal expanding outward during the striking process.

Broadstrikes are considered rare error coins, especially those with significant design details and in high grades. The scarcity of broadstrikes is attributed to the fact that they are typically caught during the minting process and removed from circulation. Collectors and error coin enthusiasts are particularly drawn to broadstrikes due to their unique appearance and limited availability.

The market demand for broadstrikes can vary depending on factors such as the coin's denomination, date, and condition. Generally, broadstrikes from popular coin series or those with notable design errors tend to command higher prices. Collectors are often willing to pay a premium for well-preserved broadstrikes that exhibit strong design details and are free from any post-mint damage.

Profiting from broadstrikes requires a keen eye for identifying these error coins and understanding their value in the market. Here are a few tips to help you maximize your profits:

1. Educate Yourself: Familiarize yourself with the characteristics and variations of broadstrikes. Study reference materials, join online forums, and attend coin shows to expand your knowledge and stay updated on the latest trends.
2. Quality Matters: Focus on acquiring broadstrikes in the best possible condition. Coins with strong strikes, sharp details, and minimal wear will always command higher prices in the market.

3. Rarity and Demand: Consider the rarity and demand for specific broadstrikes. Coins from popular series or those with unique design errors are more likely to appreciate in value over time.
4. Grading and Authentication: Have your broadstrikes graded and authenticated by reputable third-party grading services. This adds credibility and ensures potential buyers that the coin is genuine and accurately graded.
5. Market Timing: Keep an eye on the market trends and timing your sales strategically. Selling during periods of high demand or when a particular series or error type is in the spotlight can help you maximize your profits.

Brockages

Brockages are another intriguing type of error coin that occurs when a previously struck coin becomes stuck to the die and is struck again, leaving an incuse (sunken) mirror image of the original design on the opposite side. This error can occur on either the obverse or reverse side of the coin, depending on which side was stuck to the die.

Identifying a brockage error coin requires careful examination of both sides of the coin. Look for a mirror image of the design on one side, which will appear incuse (sunken) rather than raised. The brockage image may not be as sharp or well-defined as the original design, but it should still be recognizable.

Brockages are relatively rare error coins, as they occur when a coin becomes stuck to the die and is not properly ejected before the next strike. The scarcity of brockages adds to their appeal among collectors and error coin enthusiasts. The market demand for brockages can vary depending on factors such as the coin's denomination, date, and condition.Profiting from brockages follows a similar approach to broadstrikes. Here are some tips to help you make the most of your brockage error coins:

1. Research and Learn: Educate yourself about brockages and their variations. Study reference materials, consult experts, and engage with the error coin collecting community to expand your knowledge.
2. Condition is Key: Focus on acquiring brockages in the best possible condition. Coins with clear and well-defined brockage images will always be more desirable to collectors.
3. Rarity and Demand: Consider the rarity and demand for specific brockages. Coins from popular series or those with unique design errors are more likely to appreciate in value over time.
4. Grading and Authentication: Have your brockages graded and authenticated by reputable third-party

grading services. This adds credibility and ensures potential buyers that the coin is genuine and accurately graded.

5. Market Awareness: Stay informed about market trends and timing your sales strategically. Selling during periods of high demand or when a particular series or error type is in the spotlight can help you maximize your profits.

Minting Errors

Minting errors encompass a wide range of errors that occur during the minting process. These errors can be the result of mechanical issues, human error, or a combination of both. Some common minting errors include:

Off-Metal Errors

Off-metal errors occur when a coin is struck on a planchet made of a different metal than intended. For example, a nickel struck on a cent planchet or a silver coin struck on a clad planchet. These errors are highly unusual and can be extremely valuable, especially if they are authenticated and confirmed by experts.

Wrong Planchet Errors

Wrong Planchet Errors

Wrong planchet errors happen when a coin is struck on a planchet intended for a different denomination or type of coin. For instance, a quarter struck on a dime planchet or a cent struck on a foreign planchet. These errors can result in coins that are significantly undersized or oversized compared to their intended denomination.

Partial Collar Errors

Partial collar errors occur when a coin is struck with the collar only partially engaged. This can result in irregular or incomplete reeding on the coin's edge. These errors can also cause the coin to have a slightly irregular shape or a broader rim on one side.

Die Cracks and Cuds

Die cracks and cuds are errors that occur when the dies used to strike the coins develop cracks or chips. These errors can result in raised lines or blobs on the coin's surface.

Struck Through Errors

Struck Through Errors

Struck through errors occur when foreign objects, such as grease or debris, become trapped between the dies and the planchet during the striking process. These objects can leave impressions or voids on the coin's surface.

Collectors are always on the lookout for these unique and intriguing error coins. Each type of error has its own appeal and rarity, making them valuable additions to any collection. In the next section, we will explore the reasons why collectors are drawn to error coins and the benefits of collecting them.

Chapter 5

A GUIDE TO FINDING ERROR COINS IN YOUR POCKET CHANGE

Finding error coins in your everyday pocket change can be both an enjoyable hobby and a lucrative endeavor, and it's surprisingly simple to do. By adopting good habits for checking coins early on, you increase your chances of discovering valuable error coins and die varieties currently in circulation. For those seeking a greater challenge, visiting coin shows or coin shops and scrutinizing the dealer's inventory can yield new discoveries, as there are still many errors and varieties waiting to be found. However, it's essential to set realistic expectations—while valuable error coins are possible to find, they are rare for a reason. It's not uncommon to search through numerous rolls of coins without finding anything of significant value.

To begin your search, you'll need a few materials: a magnifying glass or loupe with 7X to 10X power, a good desk lamp with an incandescent bulb, a soft cloth or pad, and your daily pocket change or rolls of coins obtained from your local bank. Develop a structured approach to sorting and examining your coins, starting with grouping them by denomination. Look for abnormalities in the coin's inscriptions, date, mint mark, and primary design elements. Pay close attention to details such as die cracks, cuds, and missing elements, as well as the coin's metal composition. Be cautious of altered coins that may resemble genuine mint errors.

Examine both the obverse and reverse sides of the coin, checking for signs of doubling, missing elements, or other irregularities. Don't forget to inspect the coin's edge for any abnormalities such as seams or missing reeded edges. As you become more familiar with the process, you'll develop a keen eye for spotting potential errors quickly. Set aside any coins that appear unusual for further examination under optimal conditions.

By following these steps and practicing regularly, you can increase your chances of finding valuable error coins in your pocket change. Remember, patience and persistence are key, and each coin you examine brings the possibility of discovering a hidden treasure.

Chapter 6

PRESERVING AND CARING FOR ERROR COINS

Handling and Cleaning Error Coins

Handling and cleaning error coins is a crucial aspect of preserving their condition and value. As a collector, it is essential to understand the proper techniques and precautions to ensure the longevity of your precious error coins.

Handling Error Coins

When handling error coins, it is important to minimize the risk of damage or contamination. Here are some guidelines to follow:

1. *Wear gloves:* To prevent fingerprints and oils from transferring onto the coins, it is advisable to wear cotton gloves or use coin handling tweezers. This will help maintain the coin's surface integrity and prevent any potential damage.
2. *Handle with care:* Error coins, especially those in pristine condition, can be fragile. Avoid dropping or mishandling them, as this can lead to scratches,

dents, or other forms of damage. Hold the coin by its edges or use a soft cloth to handle it gently.

3. *Avoid excessive touching:* The more you handle a coin, the higher the chances of accidental damage. Minimize unnecessary contact to preserve the coin's condition. If you need to examine the coin closely, use a magnifying glass or a coin loupe.

4. *Keep a clean workspace:* Ensure that your workspace is clean and free from any debris or substances that could potentially harm the coin's surface. A soft, non-abrasive surface, such as a velvet pad or a clean cloth, can provide a safe area for handling and examining your error coins.

Cleaning Error Coins

Cleaning error coins is a controversial topic among collectors. While some argue that cleaning can enhance the coin's appearance, others believe that any form of cleaning can potentially damage the coin and diminish its value. It is crucial to exercise caution and consider the following points before attempting to clean an error coin:

1. *Assess the necessity:* Before deciding to clean an error coin, evaluate whether it is truly necessary. In many cases, leaving the coin in its original condition is the best course of action, as any

cleaning attempts can potentially cause irreversible damage.

2. ***Avoid harsh chemicals****:* If you decide to clean an error coin, it is crucial to use gentle cleaning methods and avoid harsh chemicals. Abrasive cleaners, solvents, or acids can cause irreversible damage to the coin's surface and should be strictly avoided.

3. ***Use mild cleaning techniques****:* For light cleaning, consider using a soft, lint-free cloth or a cotton swab lightly moistened with distilled water. Gently wipe the surface of the coin in a circular motion, being careful not to apply excessive pressure.

4. ***Patience is key****:* Cleaning error coins should be a slow and patient process. Rushing or using excessive force can lead to unintended damage. Take your time and proceed with caution, ensuring that each step is performed delicately.

Risks and Pitfalls to Avoid

While handling and cleaning error coins, it is crucial to be aware of the potential risks and pitfalls that can arise. Here are some common mistakes to avoid:

1. ***Overcleaning****:* Excessive cleaning can remove the natural toning or patina that develops on coins over time. This can significantly diminish the coin's value and desirability among collectors. Always err on the side of caution and avoid overcleaning.

2. ***Using abrasive materials****:* Abrasive materials, such as rough cloths or brushes, can scratch the surface of the coin. Avoid using any materials that can potentially cause damage. Stick to soft, non-abrasive materials for cleaning and handling.

3. ***Untrained restoration attempts****:* Attempting to restore or repair an error coin without proper training and knowledge can lead to irreversible damage. It is best to leave any restoration work to professionals who specialize in coin conservation.

4. ***Ignoring the coin's originality****:* The originality and natural state of an error coin are highly valued by collectors. Any alterations or modifications, including cleaning, can significantly impact its desirability and value. Always consider the potential consequences before making any changes to the coin's appearance.

Storage Options for Error Coins

Once you have started building your collection of rare error coins, it is essential to consider the proper storage options to ensure their long-term preservation and protection. Proper storage not only helps maintain the condition of your coins but also safeguards their value.

Coin Holders

Coin holders are one of the most popular and widely used storage options for error coins. These holders are made of inert materials such as plastic or cardboard and are designed to securely hold and protect individual coins. Coin holders come in different sizes and formats, including flips, capsules, and snap-lock holders.

Flips

Coin flips are small, rectangular plastic holders that fold in half to enclose the coin. They are an affordable and convenient option for storing individual error coins. Flips provide protection from scratches and environmental elements, and they allow easy viewing of both sides of the coin. However, they do not provide airtight protection, which may lead to tarnishing over time.

Capsules

Coin capsules are transparent, round holders made of hard plastic. They provide excellent protection against physical damage, moisture, and air pollutants. Capsules are available in various sizes to accommodate different coin diameters. They are a popular choice for valuable and rare error coins as they offer airtight protection while allowing clear visibility of the coin.

Snap-Lock Holders

Snap-lock holders are sturdy, plastic cases that securely hold the coin in place. They consist of two pieces that snap together, providing airtight protection. Snap-lock holders offer superior protection against physical damage, moisture, and air pollutants. They are an excellent option for long-term storage of valuable error coins.

Coin Tubes

Coin tubes are cylindrical containers made of plastic or cardboard that can hold a large number of coins. They are commonly used for storing bulk quantities of coins, such as those obtained from coin rolls or mint sets. Coin tubes provide a convenient and space-efficient storage solution for error coins. However, they do not offer individual protection for each coin, making them more suitable for less valuable or common error coins.

Coin Albums

Coin albums are specially designed books or binders with pages that have slots or pockets to hold individual coins. They provide an organized and visually appealing way to display and store error coins. Coin albums offer protection from physical damage and allow easy viewing of the coins without the need to remove them from the album. However, they do not provide airtight protection, which may expose the coins to environmental elements.

Coin Cabinets and Boxes

For collectors with larger collections, coin cabinets and boxes are an excellent storage option. These are typically made of wood or metal and feature multiple drawers or compartments to store and organize error coins. Coin cabinets and boxes provide a secure and visually appealing way to store and display your collection. They offer protection from physical damage and can be locked for added security.

Safety Deposit Boxes

For collectors with extremely valuable or rare error coins, a safety deposit box at a bank or a secure private vault may be the best storage option. Safety deposit boxes provide a high level of security and protection against theft, fire, and other disasters. They offer a controlled environment with constant temperature and humidity levels, ensuring the long-term preservation of your error coins. However, accessing your coins may require additional time and effort.

Environmental Considerations

Regardless of the storage option you choose, it is crucial to consider the environmental conditions in which your error coins are stored. Extreme temperatures, high humidity, and exposure to light can all have detrimental effects on the condition of your coins. It is recommended to store your error coins in a cool, dry place away from direct sunlight. Additionally, avoid storing coins near chemicals or substances that emit corrosive gases, as they can cause damage to the coins.

Insurance and Documentation

Lastly, it is essential to consider insuring your valuable error coin collection. Contact your insurance provider to discuss coverage options for your coins. It is also advisable to maintain detailed documentation of your collection, including photographs, descriptions, and any relevant certifications or grading reports. This documentation will be invaluable in the event of loss, theft, or damage, and will assist in the process of filing an insurance claim.

Preventing Damage and Tarnish

Once you have started building your collection of rare error coins, it is essential to take proper care of them to ensure their long-term preservation and value. Error coins, like any other collectible, can be susceptible to damage and tarnish if not handled and stored correctly.

Handling Error Coins

When handling error coins, it is crucial to minimize direct contact with your bare hands. The natural oils and acids on your skin can cause corrosion and tarnish over time. To prevent this, it is recommended to wear clean cotton gloves or use soft, lint-free coin handling gloves. These gloves will protect the surface of the coins from any potential damage.

Additionally, it is advisable to handle error coins by their edges rather than touching the surfaces. This will help avoid leaving fingerprints or smudges on the coins, which can affect their appearance and overall condition.

Cleaning Error Coins

Cleaning error coins is generally not recommended unless absolutely necessary. In most cases, cleaning can do more harm than good and may significantly reduce the value of the coin. The natural patina and toning on error coins are often considered desirable by collectors and can add to their overall appeal.

If you feel the need to clean an error coin, it is crucial to use gentle cleaning methods. Avoid using harsh chemicals, abrasive materials, or excessive force, as these can cause irreversible damage. Instead, consider using mild soap and warm water with a soft-bristled toothbrush to gently remove any dirt or debris. After cleaning, make sure to rinse the coin thoroughly and pat it dry with a soft cloth.

Environmental Factors

Environmental factors can have a significant impact on the condition and appearance of your error coins. Here are some important considerations to prevent damage and tarnish:

Temperature and Humidity

Extreme temperature and humidity fluctuations can cause damage to error coins. It is best to store your collection in a cool, dry place with a stable environment. Avoid areas prone to high humidity, such as basements or attics, as moisture can lead to corrosion and tarnish.

Light Exposure

Excessive exposure to light, especially ultraviolet (UV) light, can cause fading and discoloration of error coins. It is recommended to store your collection in a dark or low-light environment. If you choose to display your coins, consider using UV-filtering glass or acrylic cases to protect them from harmful light.

Air Pollution

Air pollution, particularly sulfur compounds, can accelerate the tarnishing process of error coins. It is advisable to store your collection in airtight containers or use anti-tarnish products, such as activated charcoal or silica gel packets, to absorb any harmful gases or moisture in the air.

Regular Inspection and Maintenance

To ensure the long-term preservation of your error coins, it is essential to regularly inspect and maintain your collection. Here are some recommended practices:

- Inspect your coins periodically for any signs of damage, corrosion, or tarnish. If you notice any issues, take appropriate measures to address them promptly.

- Avoid excessive handling of your coins, as this can lead to wear and tear over time.
- Keep a record of your collection, including detailed descriptions, photographs, and any relevant documentation. This will help you track the condition and value of your error coins over time.
- Consider periodically reevaluating your storage methods and materials to ensure they are still providing adequate protection for your coins.

Conservation and Restoration of Error Coins

Preserving the condition of your error coins is crucial for maintaining their value and ensuring their longevity. While some collectors prefer to keep their coins in their original state, others may choose to restore or conserve their error coins to improve their appearance or prevent further deterioration.

Understanding Conservation and Restoration

Conservation and restoration are two distinct processes that can be applied to error coins. Conservation aims to stabilize and protect the coin's condition without altering its original appearance or removing any natural toning or patina. On the other hand, restoration involves actively improving the coin's appearance by removing dirt, corrosion, or other imperfections.

It is important to note that restoration should only be undertaken by experienced professionals or individuals with a deep understanding of the process. Improper restoration techniques can irreversibly damage the coin and significantly reduce its value. Therefore, it is recommended to consult with experts or professional coin conservationists before attempting any restoration work.

Conservation Techniques

Conservation techniques are primarily focused on preventing further deterioration and stabilizing the coin's condition. Here are some commonly used conservation methods:

Cleaning

Cleaning error coins should be approached with caution, as improper cleaning can cause irreversible damage. It is generally recommended to avoid cleaning coins unless absolutely necessary. If cleaning is required, it is advisable to use mild methods such as soaking the coin in distilled water or using a soft, non-abrasive cloth to gently remove surface dirt. Avoid using harsh chemicals, abrasive materials, or excessive rubbing, as these can cause scratches or remove the coin's natural toning.

Protective Coatings

Applying protective coatings can help prevent further deterioration and protect the coin's surface. However, it is essential to use coatings specifically designed for numismatic purposes. Coin conservation professionals often use products like microcrystalline wax or archival-quality coin capsules to provide a protective barrier against environmental factors. These coatings should be applied carefully and sparingly, ensuring that they do not alter the coin's appearance or interfere with its grading.

Environmental Control

Maintaining a stable environment is crucial for preserving the condition of error coins. Exposure to extreme temperatures, humidity, or pollutants can accelerate the deterioration process. It is recommended to store your coins in a controlled environment with stable temperature and humidity levels. Avoid storing coins in basements, attics, or areas prone to fluctuations in temperature or humidity. Additionally, keep coins away from direct sunlight, as it can cause fading or discoloration.

Restoration Techniques

Restoration techniques should only be undertaken by professionals or individuals with extensive knowledge and experience in coin restoration. Here are some common restoration methods:

Surface Cleaning

Surface cleaning involves removing dirt, corrosion, or other contaminants from the coin's surface. This process requires great care to avoid damaging the coin. Professional restorers often use specialized tools and techniques such as ultrasonic cleaning, electrolysis, or chemical baths to safely remove contaminants. It is crucial to consult with an expert before attempting any surface cleaning to ensure the best possible outcome.

Re-Toning

Re-toning is a restoration technique used to recreate the natural toning or patina on a coin's surface. This process involves applying chemicals or heat to the coin to induce toning. However, re-toning should be approached with caution, as improper techniques can result in an unnatural or artificial appearance. It is recommended to seek the assistance of a professional restorer who can accurately recreate the coin's original toning.

Filling and Repairing

In some cases, error coins may have missing or damaged portions that require filling or repairing. This restoration technique involves carefully filling the damaged area with a suitable material to restore the coin's original appearance. However, it is important to note that filling or repairing error coins can significantly impact their value, especially if the restoration is not executed flawlessly. It is advisable to consult with experts or professional restorers before considering any filling or repairing work.

Seeking Professional Assistance

Given the delicate nature of conservation and restoration, it is highly recommended to seek professional assistance when dealing with valuable error coins. Professional coin conservationists and restorers have the necessary expertise, tools, and techniques to ensure the best possible outcome while minimizing the risk of damage. They can assess the condition of your error coins, provide advice on the appropriate conservation or restoration methods, and execute the necessary procedures with precision.

When selecting a professional, it is important to choose someone with a proven track record and experience in working with error coins. Seek recommendations from fellow collectors or reputable coin dealers, and inquire about their qualifications and previous restoration projects. By entrusting your error coins to a skilled professional, you can have peace of mind knowing that your coins are in capable hands.

Chapter 7

Pennies (Cents)

1955 Doubled Die Lincoln Cent

The 1955 double die Lincoln penny is one of the most famous error coins produced by the United States Mint. The doubling on the obverse is dramatic and can be seen without magnification. It is most prevalent on the date, the Motto "Liberty", and "In God We Trust". The coin's reverse was made correctly and does not exhibit any doubling.

If you think you may have found one of these coins, look at it carefully. Remember, this is not a double-struck coin.

Instead, notice that the raised detail of the coin is doubled. When a coin is double-struck, the second strike will flatten the detail from the first strike.

From the original estimate of 20,000 to 24,000 coins released into circulation, experts believe many of them got lost in circulation, and only 10,000 to 15,000 coins survive today. But occasionally, somebody finds a 1955 double die Lincoln penny while searching a roll of wheat pennies.

Value of a 1955 double die Lincoln penny: The Lincoln penny is one of the most popular series of United States Coins to collect. Due to the popularity of this coin with coin collectors, demand is very high. However, as previously stated, the supply is meager compared to the number of collectors who want to own one. Therefore, this coin is valuable in all grades.

The finest known examples have been graded MS 65 Red by PCGS, 19 coins, and MS 66 Red by NGC, one coin. Recent auction results show that a PCGS MS 65 Red example sold for $37,600 in January 2016 at a Heritage auction, while an NGC MS 66 Red example sold for over $50,000 in an August 2006 auction hosted by Superior Galleries. I am sure this coin would sell for well over $80,000 if offered at auction today. Their value ranges from around $1,800 to a whopping $125,000. The Philadelphia Mint struck them in 1955.

Based on current market trends and auction results, the estimated value range for a 1955 Double Die Lincoln penny in 2024 is:

Poor to Fair condition: $100 - $500

Good condition: $500 - $1,000

Very Good condition: $1,000 - $3,000

Fine condition: $3,000 - $10,000

Very Fine condition: $10,000 - $25,000

Extremely Fine condition: $25,000 - $50,000

Uncirculated condition: $50,000 - $100,000+ (depending on variety and grading)

1943 Copper Lincoln Cent

MS68+

Almost all 1943 pennies were made of steel due to wartime shortages. A tiny number were accidentally made of copper, making them extremely valuable (potentially hundreds of thousands of dollars!).

Check for magnet: Real copper coins don't stick to magnets, while fakes might. But be careful, some fakes are tricky!

Get it checked by an expert: Don't clean the coin, and have a professional confirm if it's real and how much it's worth.

How you authenticate your 1943 copper cent before you get to professional

You know that in 1943, bronze or copper planchet cents are extremely rare and extremely valuable. So, if you think you have one, then you need to authenticate it.

The first thing you do is weigh it. They're supposed to weigh 3.1 grams, but they can vary in weight. The one I have here weighed 2.8 grams.

The next thing that you want to do is see if it sticks to a magnet. If it sticks to a magnet, then it's a steel planchet that's coated in copper or bronze. So, this is not an authentic 1943 copper cent.

1944-S Steel Lincoln Cent (Struck on a Zinc-Coated Steel Planchet)

The 1944-S steel Lincoln cent is an intriguing WWII-era coin with significant collectible value, especially in higher grades. It provides an affordable way to own a mint error piece from a pivotal time in U.S. coinage history.

- In well-worn, circulated condition (Good-4 to Very Good-8), a 1944-S steel cent is worth $2-5.
- In lightly circulated condition (Fine-12 to Extremely Fine-40), it's valued between $5-15.
- In mint state grades, prices start increasing more substantially:
- MS-60: $20-25
- MS-63: $30-40
- MS-65: $75-100

- Higher mint state grades (MS-66 and up) quickly climb into the hundreds or thousands of dollars. MS-67 examples sell for $750-1,500 or more.
- The finest known specimens in pristine MS-68 condition can fetch $5,000-10,000+ at auction.
- The ultra rare proof versions are worth $20,000 or more, even in impaired condition.

1969-S Doubled Die Lincoln Cent

- The 1969-S doubled die is one of the most dramatic doubled die varieties in the Lincoln cent series. It is highly sought-after by variety collectors and commands huge premiums.

- In lower circulated grades, the 1969-S DDO may sell for $1,000-2,000. In mint state the values escalate quickly, with MS60 examples bringing $5,000+.

- In MS65 condition this coin sells for around $30,000-50,000 at auction. Only a few specimens have graded higher, with MS67 valued up to $125,000.

- Proofs are also known and are extraordinarily rare. Even impaired proof coins can be worth $60,000+.

- Authenticating a genuine 1969-S doubled die requires careful examination, as altered or counterfeited pieces are known. Reputable grading and certification is recommended.

1972 Doubled Die Lincoln Cent

- This variety exhibits strong doubling of the date, LIBERTY, and IN GOD WE TRUST. It is caused by hub doubling during the minting process.
- Around 250,000-500,000 of the 1972 doubled die cents were struck at the Philadelphia Mint before the error was corrected.
- While plentiful in lower grades, the 1972 DDO becomes quite scarce in uncirculated condition. It is popular with Lincoln cent variety collectors.
- In circulated grades, the 1972 doubled die may sell for $50-100. In MS60 condition it is valued around $350-500.
- In MS65 condition this variety sells for $2,000-3,000 at auction. Only a small number have been graded higher, with MS67 examples valued up to $7,500.
- Proofs are also known but extremely rare. Impaired proof specimens can still sell for $10,000+.
- Careful examination is recommended to confirm the doubling, as altered coins exist. Reputable grading/certification provides authentication.

Chapter 8

NICKELS

1937-D Three-Legged Buffalo Nickel

Mint: Denver
Obverse Designer: James Earle Fraser
Reverse Designer: James Earle Fraser

Composition: Copper-Nickel
Weight: 5g
Diameter: 21.2mm

As of February 2024, the NGC Price Guide indicates that a circulated 1937-D 3-Legged Buffalo Nickel holds a value ranging from $350 to $1950. On the open market, pristine, uncirculated specimens of this coin have been known to fetch as high as $110,000.

1950-D/S Jefferson Nickel (Over Mintmark Error)

- In well-worn, circulated grades (Good-4 through Very Good-8), a 1950-D/S Jefferson Nickel is worth around $50-75.
- In lightly circulated grades (Fine-12 through Extremely Fine-40), values are approximately $100-150.
- In Mint State grades:
- MS-60: $400-500
- MS-63: $600-800
- MS-65: $2,000-2,500
- MS-66: $4,000-6,000

- The finest known specimens in pristine MS-67 condition have sold for $8,000-10,000 at auction.

1943/2-P Jefferson Nickel (Overdate Error)

- This rare overdate was caused when a 1942 die was repunched with a 1943 date, leaving traces of the underlying 2 visible.
- It occurred exclusively at the Philadelphia mint in 1943, giving it the 1943/2-P designation.
- Only an estimated 25-40 examples of this dramatic overdate are known to exist.
- Due to its rarity, the 1943/2-P Jefferson Nickel carries enormous value in any condition.

- Well-worn Good-4 specimens have still sold for $5,000-$10,000 at auction. Even lower grade or damaged coins trade for $1,000+.
- In Mint State grades, this variety is worth a small fortune. MS-60 examples go for $50,000-$75,000. In MS-65 condition it is valued at $100,000-$125,000.
- The finest specimens grade MS-66 and have sold in excess of $200,000 in recent years.

1964-D/D Jefferson Nickel (Repunched Mintmark Error)

- In circulated grades (Good-4 through Very Good-8), the 1964-D/D is worth a small premium over face value, around $5-10.

- In lower uncirculated grades:
- MS-60: $20-30
- MS-62: $40-50
- MS-63: $50-75
- In higher mint state grades:
- MS-65: $50-100
- MS-66: $125-200
- MS-67: $300-500
- In pristine MS-68 condition, examples have sold for $1,000-2,000.
- Proofs also exist and carry a higher premium, selling for $750+ even in impaired PR-65 condition.

Chapter 9

DIMES

1942/1 Mercury Dime

The 1942/1 Mercury dime is a highly valuable overdate variety produced when leftover 1941 dime dies were repunched with a 1942 date. Only around 40-50 examples are estimated to exist. In circulated condition, values start around $2,000 and can reach $5,000+. Uncirculated specimens are extraordinarily rare - an MS-60 example may sell for $12,000-$18,000, with MS-65 grades valued up to $50,000-$75,000. The finest specimens in MS-67 have sold for over $100,000 at auction.

1968-S Roosevelt Dime No S Mint Mark

- This rare variety was caused by a few 1968 dimes being struck at the San Francisco Mint using a die that lacked the S mint mark.
- Only a handful are known to exist, with estimates ranging from 2 to 10 pieces.
- Without the S mint mark, these appear identical to the much more common Philadelphia issue from that year.
- However, its rarity makes the 1968 No S dime highly valuable to collectors and researchers.
- Even in well-circulated condition, this variety is worth $20,000-$30,000.
- Uncirculated examples are virtually unheard of. An MS-60 grade would likely trade for $75,000+.

- Proper authentication from a top grading service is highly recommended. Some altered Philadelphia 1968 dimes lack an S.

1965 Roosevelt Dime Struck on a Silver Planchet

- In 1965, the composition of the dime was changed from 90% silver to a copper-nickel clad composition. However, some dimes were erroneously struck on leftover silver planchets.
- This created 1965 dimes that contain 90% silver instead of copper-nickel, despite not having a mint mark.

- Only a small number of these errors are known, with estimates ranging from a few dozen to a couple hundred pieces.
- The silver planchet is detectable through the coin's weight, sound, and properties. Authentic examples weigh around 2.5 grams versus the normal 2.27 grams.
- In circulated condition, the variety sells for a hefty premium thanks to the precious metal value. Prices start around $1,000 and up.
- In uncirculated grades, the rarity drives values even higher. An MS65 recently sold at auction for nearly $20,000.
- Proper authentication is vital, as normal clad 1965 dimes are sometimes plated to imitate this rare mint error.

1982 Roosevelt Dime No Mint Mark

- In 1982, all dimes were struck at the Philadelphia mint. Normally they would carry a P mint mark, but a small number were issued without it.
- These "No Mint Mark" dimes lack a P below the date on the reverse side, and appear blank.
- Estimates suggest only around 10-15 of these error coins exist.
- Without a mint mark, they appear identical to the much more common proofs from that year.
- However, the rarity makes these valuable errors. In circulated grades they are worth $3,000-$5,000.
- In proof condition, they carry even more value, trading for $7,500-$10,000 in PR-65.
- Authentication by a reputable grading service is highly recommended. Some altered or counterfeit no-P dimes exist.

1996-W Roosevelt Dime (Worn Die Mint Error)

- This variety was produced at the West Point Mint facility, intended for collectors sets, but using a worn and polished die.
- On normal 1996-W dimes, the bands on the torch are crisp and well-defined. But on the worn die examples, the bands are weakened and blurred.
- Only a small number display this dramatic die wear, making it a scarce and popular mint error. Estimates range from 5,000-10,000 pieces.
- In pristine proof condition, a worn die 1996-W dime is worth around $150-300, a moderate premium.

- However, examples grading PR-69 or PR-70 can sell for up to $1,000 due to the rarity in top grades.
- Authentication of the worn die characteristics is recommended, as normal 1996-W dimes are sometimes artificially worn or impaired.

Chapter 10

QUARTERS

2004-D Wisconsin Extra Leaf Quarter

- In circulated condition, the 2004-D Wisconsin Extra Leaf quarter is worth a modest premium over face value, around $1-2.
- In lower Mint State grades like MS-60 or MS-62, it may sell for around $5-10.
- In MS-65 condition, the variety carries a more significant premium of around $50-75.
- The highest graded examples in pristine MS-67 condition have sold for $150-200 at auction.
- There are also a small number of proof versions known that can sell for $200-300 even in impaired condition.

1970-S Washington Quarter Doubled Die Obverse

- This variety shows strong doubling of the date, motto, and other obverse design elements. It was caused by hub doubling during the minting process at the San Francisco facility.
- Only a small number of the doubled die coins were struck, making it quite rare and valuable. Estimates range from 20,000-30,000 pieces.
- On average circulated examples are worth $500-1,000. Uncirculated coins carry far higher values.
- In MS-65 condition this variety sells for around $7,500-10,000 at auction. Only a few have graded higher, with MS-67 valued up to $50,000.
- Proofs also exist and are extraordinarily rare - only 5-10 proof 1970-S doubled dies are known. They trade for $100,000 or more.
- Authentication by a reputable grader is recommended. Some altered coins exist, or normal quarters with machine doubling are mistaken for the DDO.

1965 Washington Quarter Struck on a Silver Planchet

- In 1965, the quarter's composition changed from 90% silver to a copper-nickel clad. However, some 1965 quarters were mistakenly struck on leftover silver planchets.
- This produced 1965 quarters containing a full .1808 ounces of silver instead of copper-nickel, despite lacking a mint mark.
- Estimates suggest only a couple hundred or so of these rare errors were produced.
- The silver planchet can be detected by the coin's weight, resonance, and other properties. Authentic pieces weigh 6.25 grams versus 5.67 grams for clad.
- In circulated condition, the silver quarter carries a minimum value of $1,000 based on silver bullion value alone. Premiums quickly raise prices into the thousands.
- Uncirculated examples are extremely scarce and trade for at least $5,000-10,000 in MS-65 condition.

- Proper authentication is vital as altered clad quarters are sometimes plated to imitate this rare mint error.

1974-D Washington Quarter Doubled Die Obverse

- This prominent doubled die variety shows strong doubling of the date, mottoes, and Liberty's profile. It was caused by hub doubling at the Denver mint.
- It is estimated that around 4 million of the 1974-D DDO quarters were struck and released into circulation.
- While not rare in lower grades, the 1974-D DDO becomes quite elusive in high mint state grades. This increases its value for collectors.
- In circulated condition, the variety carries a modest premium in the $5-10 range. But in MS-65 condition it is valued around $175-250.
- The finest specimens grade MS-67+ and can sell for $500-1,000 or more at auction. Proofs are also known but very scarce.

- Authenticating the doubling is recommended, as normal machine doubling is sometimes mistaken for the dramatic DDO.

1983-P Washington Quarter with Doubled Die Reverse

- This variety exhibits strong doubling of the eagle, mottoes, and other reverse design elements. It is caused by hub doubling.
- The doubling is most visible on the eagle's wings, legs, and the letters of E PLURIBUS UNUM.
- It is estimated that around 10-15 million of the 1983-P DDR quarters were struck at the Philadelphia mint.
- In circulated grades, this variety carries a modest premium of $5-10 over face value. In MS-65 condition it is worth around $50-75.
- The finest specimens grade MS-67+ and have sold for $150-250 at auction. Proofs are also confirmed but very scarce.
- Authentication of the doubling is recommended, as normal machine doubling is sometimes mistaken for the true DDR.

Chapter 11

HALF DOLLARS

1970-D Kennedy Half Dollar Doubled Die Obverse

Observe	Reverse

Mint: Denver
Mintage: 2,150,000
Obverse Designer: Gilroy Roberts
Reverse Designer: Frank Gasparro

Fineness: 0.4
Weight: 11.5g
ASW: 0.1479oz
Melt Value: $3.27
Diameter: 30.6mm
Edge: Reeded

- This variety exhibits strong doubling of the date, portrait, and motto on the obverse. It was caused by hub doubling at the Denver Mint.
- It is estimated that around 200,000-300,000 of the 1970-D DDO Kennedy halves were struck.

- As of February 2024, based on the NGC Price Guide, a 1970 Kennedy Half Dollar in circulated condition is valued at approximately $3.30 to $3.80. Conversely, on the open market, 1970 D Half Dollars in pristine, uncirculated state can fetch prices as high as $12,500.
- Only a small number have been certified in top grades, making high grade specimens quite scarce and desirable.
- Authentication of the doubling is recommended, as normal machine doubling is sometimes mistaken for the true DDO.

While available in circulated grades, the 1970-D DDO Kennedy half becomes quite elusive in uncirculated condition. This significant doubled die variety carries a healthy premium in higher mint state grades.

1974-D Kennedy Half Dollar Doubled Die Obverse

- This prominent doubled die variety exhibits strong doubling of Kennedy's portrait, the date, and mottoes on the obverse. It was caused by hub doubling at the Denver mint.
- It is estimated that around 3-4 million of the 1974-D DDO Kennedy halves were struck and released.
- In circulated condition, this variety carries a modest premium in the $20-50 range. But in MS-65 condition it is valued at $175-250.
- In MS-66 condition, examples sell for around $500-750. Only a small number have been graded higher, with MS-67 valued up to $2,000.

- Proofs are also confirmed but extremely scarce, with only around 10-15 pieces believed to exist.
- Authentication of the doubling is recommended, as normal machine doubling is sometimes mistaken for the true DDO.

1976-D Bicentennial Kennedy Half Dollar with Doubled Die Obverse

- This variety displays strong doubling of the date, Liberty bell, and other obverse design elements. It was caused by hub doubling at the Denver mint.
- An estimated 10-15 million of the 1976-D DDO Bicentennial halves were struck based on the size of the mintage.
- In circulated condition, this variety carries a modest premium in the $50-100 range. In MS-65 grade it is valued around $125-200.
- In MS-66 condition, examples sell for $300-500. Only a small number have graded higher, with MS-67 pieces worth $1,000-2,000.
- Authentication of the actual doubling is advised. Normal machine doubling is sometimes mistaken for the true DDO.

- As a Bicentennial issue struck during only one year, the 1976-D DDO Kennedy half is desired by collectors assembling that special set.

1982-P Kennedy Half Dollar No Mint Mark

- All circulating 1982 Kennedy half dollars were struck at the Philadelphia mint and should bear a "P" mint mark. However, a small number were mistakenly issued without it.
- These "No Mint Mark" pieces lack a P below the date on the obverse, and appear blank instead.
- Only about a dozen or so of the 1982 No P Kennedy halves are confirmed to exist.
- Due to the very low numbers produced, this missing mint mark variety carries enormous value.
- In circulated condition, 1982 No P Kennedy halves are worth approximately $15,000-$25,000.
- In uncirculated MS-65 grade, value climbs to $50,000-$75,000 or possibly higher.
- Authentication by a reputable grading service is strongly advised for any 1982 No P Kennedy half dollar. Some altered coins may exist.

1964-D Kennedy Half Dollar Struck on a Silver Planchet

- In 1964, the composition of the Kennedy half dollar changed from 90% silver to a copper-nickel clad. However, some 1964 halves were mistakenly struck on leftover silver planchets.
- This resulted in 1964-D Kennedy halves made of solid silver instead of clad copper-nickel, despite lacking a mint mark.
- Only a small number exist, with estimates ranging from 5 to 12 pieces known.
- Their silver content makes them highly valuable. Even in circulated grades they are worth $25,000 or more.
- In uncirculated condition the value escalates significantly. An MS-65 recently sold at auction for $150,000.
- Verification of the silver composition through testing methods is essential. Some altered clad 1964 halves exist pretending to be this error.

CONCLUSION

As we've seen throughout this book, rare error coins offer tremendous excitement and reward for collectors in 2024 and beyond. While the top rarities are certainly investment-grade trophies bringing huge sums at auction, many fascinating errors are still remarkably affordable and accessible. This makes error coins ideal for collectors of all means to search for, study, and add to their cabinets.

The stories behind each mint mistake, the thrill of the hunt, and the satisfaction of owning true numismatic wonders - these passions drive error coin collectors every year. As new varieties are discovered and previously unknown specimens are unearthed, the opportunities in this field are endless.

It's my hope that this guide has provided a valuable overview of the many errors.

BONUS

COIN GLOSSARY

Alloy: A mixture of metals used to create coins.

Die: A metal stamp used to impress designs onto a coin blank.

Mint Mark: A small letter or symbol indicating the mint where a coin was produced.

Obverse: The front side of a coin.

Reverse: The back side of a coin.

Planchet: A blank metal disc ready to be struck into a coin.

Proof Coin: Specially minted coin with highly detailed relief and mirror-like fields.

Strike: The act of pressing a design onto a coin blank.

Uncirculated Coin: A coin in pristine condition, never used in commerce.

Mint Error: An irregularity or mistake during the minting process.

Luster: The shine of a coin's surface.

Grading: Evaluating a coin's condition and assigning a grade.

Numismatics: Study or collecting of coins and currency.

Face Value: The denomination stamped on a coin.

Commemorative Coin: Issued to honor a person, event, or institution.

Bullion Coin: Struck from precious metals for investment.

Edge: The outer rim of a coin.

Coin Roll: A tube containing a specific number of coins.

Double Die: A coin with doubled design elements.

Overstrike: A coin struck on top of another coin.

Mint Set: A collection of coins produced and sold by a mint.

Circulation: The process of coins being used in everyday transactions.

Commemorative: A coin issued to honor a specific event, person, or institution.

Condition: The physical state of a coin, including wear, scratches, and other imperfections.

Rarity: The scarcity of a coin, often influencing its value.

Mint State: The condition of a coin that has never been in circulation.

Proof Set: A collection of coins struck with special techniques and finishes, often for collectors.

Error Coin: A coin with a mistake made during the minting process.

Counterfeit: A fake coin made to resemble a genuine one.

Numismatist: A person who studies or collects coins and currency.

Bullion: Precious metals in the form of bars, ingots, or coins.

Numismatic Value: The value of a coin based on factors such as rarity, condition, and demand.

Legal Tender: Coins and currency that are recognized as valid for transactions by a government.

Coinage: The process of minting coins.

Toning: The natural coloration that develops on the surface of a coin over time.

Strike Quality: The precision and detail of the design on a coin.

Mintage: The number of coins produced by a mint for a specific issue.

Date: The year of issue stamped on a coin.

Design: The artwork and symbols featured on the surface of a coin.

Reeded Edge: A coin edge with raised lines or ridges, often used for security purposes.

2023 PENNY ERROR IS A MUST FIND RARITY

The 2023 Lincoln Cent with an Extra V by VDB

The most prominent error found so far shows an extra "V" punched into the lower right of the designer's initials (VDB) on the obverse shoulder. Around a dozen examples have been authenticated so far, pointing to a rare and dramatic mint mistake.

The first certified specimen graded MS67 Red sold for $152 at auction in January 2023. Other raw examples are selling for $70-100 each online in January, with prices likely to decline as more emerge. But the rarity has generated great interest.

Potential 2023 Lincoln Cent Doubled Dies

Some listings have appeared offering purported doubled die obverse 2023 cents showing possible doubling of letters and digits. These have sold in the $60-70 range on eBay, but none have been certified by major grading services yet.

While tantalizing, collectors should be wary of "doubled dies" until properly authenticated, as many fake errors exist. But with the doubled die history of Lincoln cents, new 2023 DDOs being discovered would not be a surprise.

The hunt is on among specialists to find and authenticate any 2023 Lincoln cent errors. While still early, the excitement and prices realized show the potential of discovering and owning new mint errors.

Made in United States
Troutdale, OR
09/30/2024

23252891R00096